FACE OF ADVERSITY

LIFE AS A PRISONER OF WAR

KENNETH BAILEY

Copyright Kenneth Bailey 2009
Kenneth Bailey asserts the moral right to be identified
as the author of this work.

ISBN 978-1-4092-9997-4

A catalogue record for this book is available from the British Library.

First Published in 2009 by Kenneth Bailey

Cover Design by Titanium Design Ltd.
www.titaniumdesign.co.uk

All rights reserved. No part of this publication may be reproduced, stored in a retrieval system, or transmitted, in any form or by any means, electronic, mechanical, photocopying, recording or otherwise, without the prior permission of the publishers.

*Remembering comradeship and faith
under appalling conditions – when
the best and worst elements of
human nature are revealed...*

FOREWORD BY ANDREW KENNETH WOOL

Kenneth Bailey, my Grandfather, is my hero. He is the inspiration for so much of what I do, he will never realise. I consider it an honour and a privilege that he asked me to write the foreword to his memoirs as a prisoner of war of the Japanese some 66 years ago that give a truly remarkable insight into what the unfortunate troops went through and a realisation of the devastation war brings to so many. To bring the book to print seems a fitting celebration for "Popa's" (as his grandchildren call him) 90th birthday on November 6th 2009.

Popa, as like so many who endured the same experience, never spoke about his time in the camp to his family and friends, even years down the line he still will not disclose the true horrors he saw and endured himself. It is all too painful to remember. Waking him from his nightmares was the closest my Mum and Uncles got to hear of the events. Slowly with his grandsons he opened up, first at the dinner table, telling us about the diet – or lack of – he had in the jungle and how the only protein he got was from the living maggots rummaging in the rice. It made us grateful for Nana's dinner. Perhaps that was the point?

I was small when he decided to put these thoughts on paper. By the time he had written the book and I had read it, it gave me a pure account of what my hero and his patriots went through, the monotonous routines, camp disease and hours upon hours of strenuous labour without food or water. How he stared adversity in the face and yet still managed with his fellow prisoners of war to play games against the guards for amusement.

These horrors should never be forgotten and that is why I am thankful he has written the book. Those who have been affected by or can comprehend the events will be thankful he did too. These grey days in history make sure we keep ours bright. Many gave their lives for our tomorrow.

Forever they will all be heroes. Forever he will be a hero. Forever he will be my hero.

Andrew Kenneth Wool

FACE OF ADVERSITY

CHAPTER I	Civvies to Call-up 1940.	7
CHAPTER II	On the High Seas	11
CHAPTER III	India - and into the unknown	17
CHAPTER IV	Singapore - Action!	21
CHAPTER V	Surrender and Shame	29
CHAPTER VI	Prisoners of War - enforced work under the Japanese	35
CHAPTER VII	Getting fit for hard labour - and Japanese violence	39
CHAPTER VIII	Hell-bound in railway box wagons	45
CHAPTER IX	Arrival at Bam Pong - Hell camp number one	49
CHAPTER X	Next stop Chungkai - railway building, bamboo, bashings	53
CHAPTER XI	Disease strikes, but a few camp improvements	63
CHAPTER XII	Outside help with food and medical supplies	71
CHAPTER XIII	Escape no option - environment unfriendly	77
CHAPTER XIV	Northwards to cholera and beri-beri at hell camp number two	83
CHAPTER XV	Evacuation Southwards to rumours, coffee and football!	89
CHAPTER XVI	Sailing again - Return to Singapore but no luxury trip!	95
CHAPTER XVII	Indo-China - more hard work, but good news too	101
CHAPTER XVIII	American aircraft and freedom at last	105
CHAPTER XIX	Out on the Town - meeting new friends then homeward bound	111
CHAPTER XX	Home again - thankful for survival after four lost years	119
	Postscript	125
	Ken's Diary	131
	About the Author	147

I

CHAPTER ONE

CIVVIES TO CALL-UP, 1940

My story began on 18th January 1940. I was 20 years of age and this was the day when I was called up for military service. I was told that I would be joining the 5th Battalion of the Suffolk Regiment as a "P.B.I" (Poor Bloody Infantryman - a footslogger), and was instructed to report for training at North Walsham, Norfolk. Travelling by train with other Cambridge lads so we set off on our way to fight for King and Country.

On our arrival at North Walsham, a pleasant little market town, we reported to the drill hall from where we were marched through the snow-covered streets, stopping along the way to be placed into civilian billets. Introduction to the army began immediately with parades in the drill hall for issue of uniforms; and soon we were being taught how to stand in a straight line, click our heels and salute officers. As our battalion was a Territorial Unit, we were amongst many men who were experienced soldiers and it was not long before we "rookies" began to learn from them, some of the "tricks of the trade." One piece of advice I had cause to remember for a long time was, to never leave personal army issue property lying about - to quote more specifically - "they'll pinch the laces from your boots if you're not careful." Returning from a route march one day with blisters on my feet, and having removed and left my boots to go to the far end of the drill hall for treatment to the blisters, on my return I found one of my boots laceless!

After the initial few months training in the Norfolk area, we were 'broken in' as soldiers of the King to perform guard duties at river bridges; in the sand dunes of Hemsby on coastal defence where our accommodation was in commandeered holiday bungalows,

And also in and around stately homes. We then moved on to other locations, being stationed at Fulbourn near Cambridge, then to Hawick, Scotland; Liverpool; Isle of Anglesey; and finally Leominster in Herefordshire.

It was in October 1940 that I was appointed Acting Unpaid Lance Corporal and posted to "D" Company, being granted the rank of Lance Corporal in June 1941, promotion to Acting Unpaid Corporal 3 months later and finally War Substantive Corporal. The resultant increases in pay, although small, were most welcome in providing the means to enjoy off-duty evenings a little more.

During this 18months or so of military training we were introduced to the dangerous and frightening weapons of war, at one stage taking part in a Brigade exercise where we, the infantry, had to advance under live artillery covering fire, shells from which were fired at targets in front of us as we moved forward. It was on this exercise that we experienced what could happen in real combat when a shell dropped short amongst us, resulting in a number of serious injuries and the death of a Lance Corporal comrade.

By now most of us were accustomed to this new life of being ordered about by men bearing stripes, pips and crowns on khaki uniforms. Surprisingly, everyone of we conscripts appeared to take these measures of military discipline in very good spirits, and after parades and other duties there were always evening visits to the local public houses where we could relax and curse about the sergeant major !

Apart from the stiff training we were being put through, there was always time for sporting activities, which were a must, whether one liked it or not. With football in the Winter months and mainly athletics in the Summer, these occasions were appreciated by most as a pleasant change from routine Army life. Personally, I got myself involved in any sporting event that was going, carrying on from civilian days when I played rugby, cricket and soccer, having also been a more than useful athlete in my High School days.

It was my participation in sporting activities that led to my being appointed as a physical training instructor when stationed in Hawick, Scotland. With this appointment went the issue of the treasured P.T.I.'s navy blue slacks and navy and red hooped jersey, which I was proud and privileged to possess and wear during sessions of physical training instruction. Unfortunately, the Physical Training Instructors' Command Course which had been arranged for me was cancelled, no doubt due to the fact that shortly afterwards we were granted embarkation leave, then moved to Liverpool, before the final home station move to Leominster.

In early October 1941, whilst at Leominster (at which stage we were considered to be a fully trained, most efficient and well-equipped fighting unit), we were informed that we would be going overseas, possibly for service in the Middle East, being issued with khaki drill tunics, topis and the most ridiculous sloppy, button-down over-the-knees khaki drill shorts.

FACE OF ADVERSITY

II

CHAPTER TWO

ON THE HIGH SEAS

On 27th October we entrained for Liverpool Docks there embarking on a troopship named the "Reina del Pacifico", a twin-funnelled transport as large a ship as many of us had ever seen. Supporting units of our 54th Infantry Brigade occupied other troopships, the whole forming a convoy soon to leave for what was to prove ultimately, a great misadventure. Late that evening the convoy, including an escort of British destroyers, sailed from Liverpool and headed out into the Irish Sea and Atlantic Ocean. We were made aware that we would be sailing through dangerous waters laid with mines, but the immediate journey was uneventful, except for during the first couple of days, most of the troops suffered nothing worse than bouts of seasickness.

The Reina Del Pacifico

Five days sailing time out from Liverpool we awoke in the morning to see a mass of ships approaching which we were told was a convoy of merchants bound for England; this convoy being escorted by a fairly large American fleet of warships. In mid-ocean the fleet manoeuvred so that it had turned in a position to be then escorting our troop ships. Meanwhile the warships, which had escorted us from Liverpool, turned around heading back to England with the merchants. (It is worth noting that America did not enter the war as our allies, officially, until 8th December 1941!)

Reina del Pacifico

Eventually, on 8th November, we docked at Halifax, Nova Scotia, on the Canadian eastern seaboard, there disembarking the "Reina del Pacifico" to board an American troopship, once an ocean-going cruise liner, of 40,000 tons named the Wakefield. Compared to the previous ship this was a magnificent looking transport, everything about it being first class, accommodation and food excellent and friendliness of the American crew could not have been better. After allocation of deck and bunk hammock spaces, the next day we set sail, together with two other similar troopships, the Mount Vernon and the West Point, both former American luxury liners of similar tonnage to the Wakefield and carrying the 53rd Infantry Brigade, the convoy being escorted by American warships, including an aircraft carrier "The Saratoga".

Leaving Halifax sailing south along the Eastern coast of America we arrived at Port of Spain, Trinidad on 17th November for the purpose of refuelling and stock replenishment, which was carried out in the harbour without docking; so no shore leave here. On 19th our journey continued onward, crossing the Equator eastwards towards Cape Town, South Africa.

After almost three weeks sailing from Trinidad, on 9th December our convoy neared Cape Town's Table Bay, on the approach to which we were afforded a most wonderful sight of the phenomenal Table Mountain on the horizon. To the time our ship tied up at the docks everyone was amazed at the striking panorama which was revealed, and we were even treated to the apparently unusual sight of a "cloth" on the " Table" formed by a layer of white cloud suspended above it.

Here at Cape Town in glorious warm weather, we enjoyed three days shore leave, most of the troops being met at the docks by local people and being invited to their homes for meals. We soon became aware of the dissociation between the white and black South Africans when we travelled about the town, the 'whites' seemingly keeping entirely to themselves, there being very few signs of friendly connection with the black Africans. Later of course, this situation worsened so that there was much racial segregation leading to apartheid in South Africa.

During our walks in the centre of Cape Town we marvelled at the huge skyscraper office blocks, the like of which most of us had not seen before. From the sky-high windows of these imposing buildings as we walked the streets, we were greeted with waving hands and handkerchiefs from the occupants of the offices.

At this time we were still under the impression that we were due for action in the Middle East, but soon we were to learn that Pearl Harbour had been attacked by the Japanese and that America was now involved in the war ! We were told that our immediate destination was to be India, and so we were convinced that, despite having been issued with uniform and equipment for desert use, the Middle East was not for us.

After leaving Cape Town on 13th December we enjoyed wonderful days sailing in deep blue waters of the Indian Ocean; with cloudless skies and endless horizons, lapping up the brilliant sunshine, taking in the astonishing colours of the tropical sunrises and sunsets, and also experiencing the easygoing leisurely activities on board. Each day usually began with early morning physical training. My job as platoon P.T.I was taking the men in early morning exercises, always including a few laps around the long and spacious deck. Boxing training took place also, as did organised boxing matches between the different British units and the American crew, in which our boys acquitted themselves exceptionally well.

Apart from these fitness activities, much of the leisure time each day was spent on deck soaking up the sun and being thoroughly engrossed in watching the manoeuvres of the escort ships. Often at these times we had also watched the antics of the flying fish and porpoise, something else which most of us had not witnessed before. Despite the knowledge that we were heading for active service, I am sure that most of us were enjoying the experience on this super cruise ship, albeit that sleeping accommodation was in canvas hammocks and we were still under strict disciplinary orders.

The realisation that we were now very much a part of the war became apparent when the ship's alarm would sound and we had to don lifejackets and muster on deck for practice lifeboat drill. There were times when the necessity for these practices became obvious; that was when enemy submarines were believed to be operating in the area, and these were occasions when our escort vessels would circle the convoy dropping depth charges. The result of this action was the sounds of the underwater explosions with resultant vibrations of the ship, and fortunately nothing worse.

This chapter of our journey abroad brings back memories of all the luxuries which were on offer on the ship - American sweets and chocolate, cartons of Chesterfield and Camel cigarettes, cigars and many other commodities - many of which were not available on our previous ship. There were no complaints either concerning the food provided by the Yankee cooks, nor the fact that having collected our rations on steel trays, we then ate the food whilst standing up at long, narrow benches; no seating or tables being provided. As Christmas Day 1941 arrived and was celebrated on board, we enjoyed turkey, tasty ham and Christmas cake - of course all in typically large American portions!

Whilst enjoying the easy-going, generally tranquil life on board, one incident marred the pleasures we had so far been enjoying when a member of the troops fell ill, sadly died and had to be buried at sea.

After this man's death, and leading up to his burial, it was noticed that sharks were closely following our ship. The story told by those experienced sea travellers on board was that these creatures of the deep somehow sensed when death had occurred at sea and that it was not unusual for them to trail ships in such circumstances. It was also said that in such instances, and just before sea burials, sides of meat from ships' galleys would be thrown overboard in order to entice the sharks away from the ships. Only old 'Sea Dogs' know if these gruesome stories are true! Most of us had spent hours watching the sharks, which were plainly visible just beneath the surface of the clear ocean and following very closely in the wake of the ship. We had been intrigued and surprised that the sharks continued in pursuit for such a long time; everyone concluding that there was some truth in the stories related by the ship's crew.

III

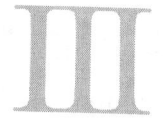

CHAPTER THREE

INDIA – AND INTO THE UNKNOWN

Our next port of call was Bombay, which was reached on the morning of 27th December, and now we guessed that we were bound more likely for Singapore, and most assuredly not the deserts of the Middle East. Having disembarked at Bombay we boarded a train, the carriages of which were utterly dirty, having hard wooden seating with no upholstery whatsoever. The toilets, such as they were, being merely holes in the flooring above which users squatted or stood. As far as can be remembered, we were given no specific information as to where we were going, nor for how long we would be travelling, and speculations ran high.

After a long, overnight and most uncomfortable journey, we arrived at Ahmadnagar, a small market town, and here we encamped at a former Indian Army barracks. The buildings in which we were to be accommodated here were quite substantial with the arid, dusty barrack square being centrally situated.

It soon became clear that this stage of our overseas service was the introduction to living it rough; the barrack rooms themselves being far from clean and having a definite Asian atmosphere about them. Our beds were four-legged, rickety wooden frames with fibre-latticed bases and straw-filled mattresses on solid wooden bases. Despite the crudeness of these structures they gave us reasonable comfort, particularly when we were tired out after training and route marches in the scorching heat. It was during these times when we were on our beds, if we were not asleep, that we saw for the first time, friendly lizards traversing the walls and ceilings snapping at the troublesome mosquitoes, a menace which most of us had not encountered before.

As well as keeping fit by route marches, during which we saw thousands of enormous bats hanging upside down from tree branches, we continued with really hard training, and we also played one or two football matches on grassless, dusty pitches against other Army units. Half-time for the players at these matches was spent with parched throats and everybody gasping for breath. It was so hot and airless, and we were grateful for the sweet tea provided by native boys during the half-time breaks and at the end of the matches. Apart from these activities, we were involved in guard mounting, field training and company drill, and on the two Sundays spent here, attending church parades.

Our off-duty evenings here at Ahmadnagar were now and again taken up with trips to the local bazaar in a horse-drawn cart driven by a local Indian but, apart from our interest in the living habits of the Indians here, and native goods for sale in rather ramshackle shops, these excursions were hardly worth the trouble and time.

Back at the barracks, each morning as dawn broke we were awakened by the call of an Indian tea-maker ("Char Wallah, Sahib!"), who was allowed into the camp to sell his hot sweet tea to the troops. It was the opinion of us all that this native's tea was far tastier than that dished up by our own cookhouse, and it was considered well worth being woken up for at such an early hour.

Our camp food, typical army style stuff, with bully beef to the fore, we collected from the cookhouse situated across the padang (barrack square), some 50 to 80 yards away from our huts. Each trip from the cookhouse to the huts was an expedition fraught with considerable danger. Setting out with our food-laden plates or mess tins to return to the huts we were "dive-bombed" by huge, ravenous black hawks which swooped upon us to snatch the food from the utensils in our hands. These were very strong birds that dived at tremendous speed, and many a soldier lost his rations as a result of their attacks, sometimes having his plate or mess tin knocked from his hands as the hawks made contact. The only way of protection

INDIA – AND INTO THE UNKNOWN

from these onsets was to cover the food before leaving the cookhouse and making the journey between there and our huts at a fast pace, keeping a very firm grip on our food utensils.

It was now January 1942 and we had supposedly been regaining fitness with all the route marches, training exercises and sport after our long sea trip from England. So on 14th January we departed Ahmadnagar, rejoined our ship at Bombay the next day, eventually sailing off for Singapore on 19th, being told - as if we were not already aware - that we were to prepare to do battle against the Japanese. During this part of our journey, brief instructions concerning jungle warfare were issued, and also talks on such subjects as habits of the Japanese, and ability to identify Japanese from Chinese men by their facial features. Advice was also given on how to guard against contracting malaria, and how to protect against mosquito bites by using the vile, strongly odorous Army Issue mosquito cream. (After the battle for Singapore some Japanese troops were reported to have stated that during the conflict they were able to locate the British troops because of the smell of the cream !) Another interesting talk given to us, of a non-military nature for a change, was by that famous cricket commentator and journalist, E.W.(Jim) Swanton, who was also one of us heading for service in the East. The topic of Jim Swanton's talk was a most fascinating one of his experiences with English county cricket and test matches around the world.

Now on the high seas again, sailing South back into the Indian Ocean, we headed East towards our final destination. As our convoy approached Singapore in line through the narrow Banka Straits, a single Japanese 'plane attacked unsuccessfully, its bombs surprisingly missing what appeared to be an easy target of some twelve ships. From my position high up on the top deck of our ship the Wakefield, which was fourth in line, spouts of water could be plainly seen as the bombs missed the ships behind the Wakefield, and fell into the sea. We all now had an awareness that the war zone was not very far off.

FACE OF ADVERSITY

IV

CHAPTER FOUR

SINGAPORE – ACTION!

On disembarking at Singapore on 29th January, we saw that another ship was about to leave the docks when we were surprisingly informed that on board were the remnants of the R.A.F. which were leaving the island to take up station on Java. At the very time of disembarking we were under attack from Japanese aircraft, and with the knowledge that the R.A.F. were leaving the island, it was unmistakably and painfully obvious, although not readily admitted, that we were doomed.

Having landed on the island of "The Impregnable Fortress" some of the units of our 18th Division had gone straight into action in Malaya in support of the mainland force, the remainder of us occupying part of the island's defences. Our battalion's first encampment on the island was in a rubber plantation where we occupied tents and where we had as camp neighbours, soldiers of the Ghurkha regiment. It was here that we saw the method used to tap the raw rubber from the trunks of the rubber trees. Around the trunks of the trees, some two or three feet from ground level, earthenware cups were strapped, into which the raw rubber slowly dripped from the "V" shaped incisions in the tree bark above.

In the days that were to follow, our situation became increasingly hopeless, as did the position of the Singapore population. With the exodus of the R.A.F. the morale of the defending troops was obviously sinking lower by the hour. To further the anguish, there was distressing news that Japanese forces were making swift descent through Malaya. It seemed that those of us on the island would have to just await the outcome of the rearguard action which was taking place in the South of Malaya by the British, Australian, Indian and Malayan troops. This combined force had fought valiantly from Northern Malaya, always it seemed, against tremendous odds, the enemy appearing to have been well trained in jungle warfare and apparently being backed up by superior numbers of artillery, aircraft and mechanised units.

Our battalion eventually took up a position in the North East of the island where we suffered our first casualties caused by Japanese mortars which were operating from Southern Malaya. At this time it seemed that our troops were still endeavouring to stem the tide of enemy advance on the Malayan mainland whilst they were being continually attacked, not only by ground forces, but by Japanese aircraft, artillery and mortar fire too.

At my platoon's position at Ponggol Point, which overlooked the mile-wide Straits of Johore between Singapore and the South Coast of Malaya, we could plainly see enemy movements opposite and it was obvious that they too were aware of our position. Little wonder that we were tied down by mortar fire for much of the time whilst occupying this position, and it was here that two men of our battalion were mortally wounded by mortar shrapnel.

Our accommodation here at Ponggol Point was in a deserted Chinese house set amongst palms, banana and pineapple crops, the sparse furnishings in the house being typically Asian. Now and again we would have the company of large black pigs that were forever chasing around the open yard; and on one occasion a zebra which had strayed from the local zoo, somehow found itself in the vicinity, to be ridden bareback by one of the troops. These un-warlike activities of course taking place between mortar bombardments.

Our platoon situation here at Ponggol Point was right on the waters edge immediately facing the Malayan Johore Straits coastline. The only defences we found here were bundles of empty tin cans strung along and suspended on wire just above the waterline; this rudimentary system supposedly to serve as an audible alarm against the enemy making landings at night. (Ponggol Point Beach was later to be the burial ground for hundreds of Chinese Singapore residents, rounded up by the Japs after Singapore fell, murdered and buried on this beach . When the allies reoccupied Singapore and Malaya in 1945 the hunt began by Allied investigators to identify and bring to trial the Japanese perpetrators of this, and many other similar atrocities which the Japanese committed against the Chinese.)

Although it seemed that our overall situation was far from being tenable, nevertheless the local newspapers brought down to us by a Malayan resident bore the headlines, "The skies over Singapore will be black with 'planes tomorrow." This message of so-called comfort was purported to have been sent by Winston Churchill in an endeavour to rally the Allied Forces. As it happened that statement turned out to be correct, but the 'planes were Japanese bombers in their usual formation of 27 at a time, dropping bombs, unmolested by British fighters. The only friendly 'planes we had seen since our occupation of the island were Vildebeeste and Brewster Buffalo, both ageing aircraft which we had never seen in actual combat.

As our situation became progressively worse, so we were withdrawn to the area of Bukit Timah Road some miles South West, this new position now considered being the front line. Moving into the battle area I recall that as we did so we were offered and handed some "chapattis" by an Indian who was frying them at a stall by the side of the road. Although the Indian's intention was appreciated, there were very few of us who enjoyed or fully consumed this strange, tasteless, flat pancake-type bread. It seemed at the time that the Indian was feeling some concern for us as we were about to take up our position, and a few of us gave a thought that this food might be the last for some time to come.

In our new position we were now realising that we were in a very serious situation, being informed that our mainland troops were about to retire to Singapore after which the Johore Causeway between the mainland and Singapore island was to be destroyed. Shortly we were to suffer utter dejection on hearing in the distance, the bagpipes of the Argyll and Sutherland Highlanders leaving the mainland on the retreat from Malaya across the Causeway, which soon was to be mined and blown, but as we later learned, unsuccessfully so.

We had not long to wait before we were given the fateful news that the Japanese now had a foothold on the island, (so much for the destruction of the Johore Causeway which purpose was, to delay the enemy's advance!) At the same time we were ordered by our Company Commander to "bayonet charge the b——s if they come this way." As well as this command, we were also given a frightening instruction that we should shoot anybody, male or female, we might see moving about our area and who we suspected might be Japanese in disguise. This was the time when we realised that we were really involved in combat, and opined if we could now earnestly put into practice all that which we had been trained to do during the past two years.

On a number of occasions whilst in our battle positions, we saw persons who appeared to be natives wander across our front driving cattle, and of course, bearing in mind the warning about Japs being in disguise, they were treated with some suspicion in the serious situation we were now facing. It was hard to believe that those persons, if they were local Singaporeans, would venture into an active battle area in this way, and so necessary action had to be taken. How many of such persons became casualties, albeit perhaps being innocents, will never be known. Such were the tragedies of war.

We received no other orders or instructions concerning battle plans or enemy troop movements at this time. In fact, as a Section we, and without doubt the rest of our Platoon, felt completely isolated and unattached. Another disheartening happening was the sight of clouds of smoke billowing from oil tanks set on fire by British troops in a "scorched earth" policy to prevent them from falling into Japanese hands. It was so obvious at this time that our troops on the ground, the infantrymen, were getting no support at all from mechanised units. The truth was that we were not aware of the existence of even light tanks, and we were at a complete standstill. On two occasions only did we see bren gun carriers moving around; tanks in support might have given us some hope, but this was not to be. It seemed that we were simply a body of unprotected foot soldiers without any support, just awaiting the inevitable.

Our position at Bukit Timah Road was amongst trees and mangrove shrubs just a short distance in front of Raffles' College, which was our Battalion Headquarters. It was whilst in this position that we were subjected to attack by machine gun and rifle fire, and also by mortar bombs. It was said that the Japanese mortar bombs contained explosive crackers, and this seemed to be so as they burst with infernal noise and flashes on contact with the ground. There was also worrying news that the enemy were using dumdum bullets, missiles that we had learned expanded on impact. It was not hard to imagine what terrible injuries such bullets could cause to a human body, although under our circumstances at the time, little thought was given to the news.

Resulting from this ensuing onslaught, two of our Company stretcher-bearers lost their lives in going to the aid of men who had been injured in the attack. During one such mortar raid the earth shook, and at the same time we heard a thud as a bomb landed in the soft mangrove swamp just in front of our Section Bren gun; the partly embedded missile being clearly visible to us all, but no explosion followed . We could do nothing but just wait there with no chance of moving our position for fear of becoming easy, open targets. We could only hope that the bomb was faulty; luckily this proved to be the case and it remained inactive.

After a night of almost continual attack by Japanese fire, accompanied by screams of the injured and dying, the morning of Sunday 15th February 1942 dawned with no indication that our situation might improve. News came to us that the water supply on the Island had been severed, and also that the civilian population and the City were being heavily bombed. With the thought of no water being available one member of my Section, a short, thickset tough Irishman, Private Carroll, said that he would try to find something to drink. In our current situation there was no reason to deny him his request. Off he crawled, rifle in hand disappearing in the direction of Raffles' College and the deserted civilian houses behind us.

Some minutes after Carroll's departure, the jangling of glassware was heard, and there crawling back along a malarial drain and through the mangrove roots was the little man himself. Reaching us he produced from inside his tunic, bottles of gin and whisky that he said he had found in an empty house. Although our situation did not warrant it, nor did we feel it to be a time for drinking the 'hard stuff', we were grateful to Carroll, and pleased to just mildly slake our thirsts.

At this time, and for the past few hours, we had been aware of an air balloon, which we understood to be a Jap observation balloon, hovering above and close to our position. In a normal wartime situation with adequate support of fighter planes or artillery, such a target would not have survived, but it was not threatened at all, much to the dismay of the troops. Consequently, we felt that any move we might make would have been under enemy scrutiny and so we were tied down completely in this very confined area of tangled mangroves.

Although as a section we were out on a limb, with no orders, instructions or support from officers for hours, the men of my section amazingly maintained a calm, true disciplined temperament throughout this trying situation. Such cool character remained despite the fact that we were constantly aware of the presence of that potentially dangerous, unexploded bomb in our midst, as well as the possibility of attack from and confrontation with the enemy.

FACE OF ADVERSITY

V

CHAPTER FIVE

SURRENDER AND SHAME

During that late afternoon from our Section position, we saw, some few hundred yards in front of us, a small convoy of open military vehicles moving away to our left. It was very plain to us that in one of these vehicles a Union Jack was being held aloft by someone, and in another a large white flag was displayed. Later that day we were given the order to lay down our arms as Singapore had surrendered. As a result, being somewhat confused and disheartened, we disposed of our rifles, machine guns, small arms ammunition and grenades by dropping them in the malarial drains and amongst the mangroves. Our unit later retired into Raffles' College where we found food and drink, and where we also found beds and white sheets and pillows. That night we spent fairly comfortably, although with some trepidation, not knowing what was to become of us in the morning with the arrival of our captors-to-be.

Now was the time for reflection and realisation that we, the 5th Battalion of The Suffolk Regiment, a unit of a Brigade considered to be a most efficient and well-trained fighting force, had travelled 20,000 miles simply to surrender. The culpable lack of information, instruction and physical back-up support whilst occupying our front line disposition meant that we were absolutely static. In that situation we were given no chance to prove our worth in actual combat. How different things would have been had we received the logistic support which we might have expected, but which only the enemy appeared to have.

Next day we were assembled in the grounds of the College where we saw for the first time a close-up of our captors; a bunch of scruffy, slant-eyed little men, many of them bespectacled, dressed in dirty green uniform, rubber shoes, peaked caps and wearing puttees up to their knees. To say that we were humiliated by what we were seeing as victors in a conflict against a supposedly top class army as ourselves, would be a gross understatement. We were all naturally ashamed and disgusted, although knowing that from the very outset, we had lacked the necessary support.

Now came the official order that all weapons were to be handed over to the enemy, followed by much activity between our officers and the Japanese. That night we spent sleeping out in the open, bedded down on the grass at the rear of the College, and wondering what was in store for us.

The next day, 17th February, after a conference between our commanding officer and the Japanese we were ordered to form up as a unit and told that we were to march with other groups to Changi some 15 miles to the North East. As a result, at 5pm that day we set off in our thousands, feeling desperately degraded, being escorted by Jap guards, some on bicycles, others walking, and some Japanese officers in cars. En route we passed numerous dead bodies, many of them of non-combatants, which lay by the roadside and in the malarial drains, these bodies being swollen with the heat, covered with flies and causing a terrible stench. Our journey also took us past the now infamous Changi prison when we observed inmates waving to us from the tiny cell windows. At the end of the march that night we all slept by the roadside, to continue our trek at 6.30 the next morning.

At the end of a long, hot march, at 11am on 18th we reached our destination at Changi, a pre-war garrison, where we encamped, first in the playing field area, then amongst coconut trees. Here we began making bivouac out of gas capes, ground sheets and anything else we could find to give shelter from the anticipated heavy rains. It was whilst amongst the coconut trees I recall that on two or three occasions during the night, coconuts were heard to fall from the trees. As the coconuts made contact with the ground there would follow the sounds of hurried footsteps as men rushed from their bivouacs to get to the coconuts first. We were all endeavouring to scavenge for anything edible even at this early stage of our captivity!

Of course it did not take too long for the jokers amongst us, with typically British Army humour, to wait for dead of night silence and then to simulate the thud of a coconut hitting the ground. The resultant sound of scurrying footsteps, followed by the offensive expletives of those who had been deceived, were received with great glee by the successful pranksters. This was true British wit in the face of the seriousness of being taken prisoner less than 48 hours before, and much of this spirit was to remain through the coming months and years despite the worsening of events during incarceration.

Soon we moved from our bivouacs in the open to occupy the barracks, which were strong well-built buildings containing solid wooden beds, but very little else. Unfortunately the ablution arrangements were inadequate because of the earlier severance of the water supplies to the island. Also, due to the concentration of so many prisoners in such a small area, it was necessary for us all to be engaged in the digging of latrines within the camp. It was not long before these latrines out in the open became health hazards due mainly to the prevailing heat, so attracting mosquitoes and flies, and subsequently millions of maggots.

It was now that we were hearing stories about the inhuman behaviour of the Japanese troops, bearing out the history of their violation of the Chinese when Japan began their expansion plans in 1937 with the intention to advance into Indo-China, South East Asia and the Pacific. We were also getting information of more recent atrocities committed by the Japanese on inmates at Alexandra Hospital in Singapore where patients had been massacred, some whilst on operating tables, and also where nurses and other hospital staff had been bayonetted by the marauding invaders.

So far, at least for the first few days, we were unaware of the actual presence of our captors within the camp and we were getting somewhat organised under the command of our own officers. For the first two or three days here at Changi we were able to go swimming at the beach, albeit usually in oily waters. Even now we were beginning to feel the pangs of hunger with rations of food diminishing fast, although so far we were leading a fairly sedentary time and could just about survive so long as we had no exhaustive activities in which to concern ourselves.

As time went on it was considered necessary to maintain discipline amongst the prisoners and so British officers began to organise working parties to carry out tasks within the camp for the benefit of everyone. Lack of food was now becoming a serious problem, our own supplies running out, and it was then a question of our officers appealing to the Japanese to provide some. As a result, on 24th February, sacks of rice were sent in, and this unfamiliar food was to comprise our staple diet, (most unpalatable compared to our customary versatile potato.) Although the prospect of rice as our principal food did nothing for taste buds, we had to endure it, endeavouring to turn a blind eye to the presence of weevils and maggots mingled with the filthy grains. With our new diet, we found that, although after consuming the rice our stomachs felt full and bloated, hunger was appeased only for a short time before liquidization by natural bodily functions quickly brought on the discomfort of emptiness again.

It did become possible to procure from various sources, coconuts, bananas and pineapples, together with a little sugar which, when mixed with the infested rice at least concealed the distasteful mess which we were going to have to stomach for a long time to come. Of course, the poor quality of this so-called food was bound to take its toll and as early as the first few days of captivity men began to suffer from the effects of malnutrition and vitamin deficiency, resulting in many cases of severe diarrhoea and skin complaints. Sick parades became inevitable and the medical officers had to administer treatment as best they could without the necessary medicines promised by the Japanese, but which so far, had failed to materialise.

VI

CHAPTER SIX

PRISONERS OF WAR – ENFORCED WORK UNDER THE JAPANESE

As well as jobs within the camp area for our own benefit, working parties of prisoners were now being demanded by the Japanese for tasks in and around Singapore, with such jobs as clearing bomb damage in the City centre and work on the docks. Although some of the work was very hard and tiring at times for many of the prisoners, quite often there were opportunities to turn these labours into profitable and beneficial excursions, with food mainly in mind of course.

Apart from fruit and eggs passed to prisoners furtively by friendly Chinese, there were times, especially when working in and around the godowns (warehouses), on the docks to pilfer from stocks of foodstuffs there.(Yes, we quickly all became thieves for the sake of our stomachs, and why not, we were only stealing from the enemy, food which was once part of our own reserve stocks.)

On one such occasion when working on the docks, boxes containing jars of Marmite were found, and despite the usual body searches by the Japanese guards at the end of the day, amazingly the Marmite was smuggled aboard the lorry transport and ended up back in camp, being a vital asset for the sick, and so providing the important vitamin B already so lacking in our diets.

By now we all knew that the guards would not tolerate anything that might cause trouble for themselves with resultant disciplinary action against them by their senior officers. We were also aware that the risks involved in stealing, and any similar acts by prisoners, were more than likely to bring down the wrath of the guards upon the transgressors if such acts were discovered. Despite this, British soldiers were always ready to take risks if the successful result of these was likely to be beneficial to health. One other such act of appropriation is recalled.

When having finished work on the dockside one evening and lined up ready for tenko, (Japanese for parade, roll-call), prior to boarding lorries to return to camp, I noticed that one of our party in the line-up in front of me seemed agitated and suffering some discomfort. The Japanese guard at this time was carrying out the roll-call in the usual way by checking and counting the prisoners from the front row; it was then that I saw the reason that was causing the distress to the man in front of me. A trickle of brown greasy matter was slowly emanating from his nether region under his shorts, inch by inch down the back of his legs. Those of us in the rear rank guessed what was happening; as our friend also knew only too well. We were concerned that the guard might walk behind the front rank in the process of counting those of us in the rear prior to boarding the lorries for return to camp, in which situation he would have had the same view as we. As luck would have it the guard was satisfied from his position at the front that we were all present, and we prepared to board the lorries. As we moved towards the transport we closely surrounded our friend making sure that the guard could not see him, and we succeeded in getting him aboard without notice.

The reason for this scare was caused by our friend's body heat melting the contents of a stolen package of Ghee, an Eastern type of cooking fat, which was a very useful additive to our diet. We often came across 4 gallon tins of this Ghee when working on the docks and, when opportunities arose, we would steal small portions of the fat, wrap them in pieces of sacking or whatever else was handy, and conceal them on our person. This is exactly what our friend had done on this occasion by tucking his pack of stolen fat down his shorts, with the resultant melting and liquidization of the Ghee.

PRISONERS OF WAR – ENFORCED WORK UNDER THE JAPANESE

There was no doubt that our friend had come close to what could have resulted in a very violent end, had his act been discovered by the guard. As it turned out, it was certainly a 'sticky end' for him !

FACE OF ADVERSITY

VII

CHAPTER SEVEN

GETTING FIT FOR HARD LABOUR – AND JAPANESE VIOLENCE

As time went by British officers realised that it was necessary for prisoners to keep their minds active in educational and social subjects, so classes were organised and attended by many in after-work hours. It was also at about this time when the Japanese decided that all prisoners should keep fit by doing physical training, and so two to three hundred of us were paraded on the barrack square. The Japanese Officer in charge called for a British physical training instructor to go up on to the improvised rostrum to instruct and perform the necessary exercises. It seemed that I was the only P.T.I. there and I was ordered up to the rostrum where a Japanese instructor and an interpreter demonstrated the exercises I was to give to my colleagues. As it happened the exercises were not in any way vigorous or physical, mainly easy deep breathing exercises, which surprised, and certainly pleased the troops of course.

After a short time at the barracks a party of us was moved to a small, former R.A.F. camp situated close to the Singapore Bukit Timah Golf Club and adjacent to the McRitchie Reservoir. The huts at this camp, all ground floor buildings, were rather dilapidated having the appearance that the former occupants had attempted to destroy everything within. In the absence of any kind of furniture we all searched around in order to find anything that would help to make the place more habitable. As a result, bed frames were fashioned from timber; sacking or other material, which could be found being utilised as mattresses or blankets. In the same vicinity, some under canvas, fellow prisoners from the Norfolk regiment, Cambridgeshires and other units joined us to await whatever the Japanese had in store for us.

It was soon that we were to learn that our job here was to build a shrine on a hill on the far side of the Reservoir, apparently in honour of the Japanese troops who had perished on the island. This assignment first entailed digging up the fairways and greens of the golf course to make roads leading to a wooden bridge, which was being built over the reservoir by other prisoners. The roads having been completed, the next step was to build a walkway from the foot of the hill on the other side of the reservoir up to the site of the proposed shrine at the summit.

This was not an unpleasant job, we having now become accustomed to enforced manual work. Most of the time the weather was fine and very, very hot. Our food, still mainly boiled rice, was necessarily becoming more acceptable, at times with the addition of fruit - bananas and pineapples - and some eggs. These items could be purchased from native Malays or Chinese who now and again were allowed up to the site perimeter. The only fly in the ointment here regarding our working conditions, was the Japanese officer in charge who, at times could be quite pleasant, especially when talking about the time he had spent at college in England before the war. Nevertheless when he considered that the job we were doing was not satisfactory we saw the very unpleasant side of him that caused him to become a most belligerent, cudgel-wielding raving maniac.

Also here we encountered a typically hateful guard who we called 'Changi Joe'. He too was prone to occasions when he went absolutely berserk, hitting out at anyone in range, as did the other guards whenever the slightest opportunity arose. It was at this stage that we became aware that most of the guards were in fact Koreans, and we were soon to find that those guards themselves were sometimes given a hard time by the Japanese guards and officers. Now we all realised that taking any kind of risk in provocation against

GETTING FIT FOR HARD LABOUR – AND JAPANESE VIOLENCE

the guards was not in our best interests, having already heard of, and seen enough instances of their primitive and barbaric actions against prisoners. By this time most of us realised that survival depended upon how sharp-witted and clever we were in appearing to do the work as ordered, but doing no more; and much less whenever this was possible.

Before the completion of this particular job we received Red Cross parcels, believed to have been sent from South Africa. These contained powdered soup, chocolate and cigarettes, and some tropical topi style hats. We of course still had to eat rice as the main meal and whatever else the cookhouse men could muster, with the luxury of the parcel foods as a welcome addition. There were many of us who had nothing from which to eat our meals as mess tins and cutlery were left behind on capitulation, and so on our trips to the work sites many of us were on the lookout for anything that would ensure that we did not miss out on our rations. In this respect, sometimes we could be lucky and come across hub discs from abandoned, or otherwise available motor vehicles, which when cleaned up, made excellent food dishes; really 'state of the art' utensils !

Many hours, whether at work or resting, were spent wondering how our folks at home were coping with the war, especially with regard to food rationing. We used to ponder as to what sort of meals they might be eating and how much the quality of their food might now have deteriorated. This subject caused many of us to wish that we could now partake of our favourite meals,(my particular choice always included apple pie and clotted cream, as it still does today.) Naturally, food was uppermost in our minds, as too were hopes that there might be some truth in the many rumours that we were hearing every day, that the war would soon be over and those meals would become realities again.

Another important part of our lives now was the necessity for personal bodily cleanliness to guard against contracting disease, as well as for comfort after toiling in the tropical sun. As there were no facilities here for baths or showers of any kind, when the storms came, accompanied by the monsoon rains, off came our shirts, shorts or "G" strings and we were outside the huts to enjoy the luxury of the cool refreshing rain on our bare bodies. In the circumstances, with no civilians in the vicinity, there was no fear of embarrassing anyone, nor feelings of any shame in our undressed state out in the open.

FACE OF ADVERSITY

CHAPTER EIGHT

HELL-BOUND IN RAILWAY BOX WAGONS

In October 1942 came the announcement from the Japanese, that all prisoners were to leave Singapore to travel to Thailand where they would occupy a Red Cross camp with hot and cold running water, no work, and plenty of good food. By this time we had become accustomed to broken Japanese promises and so nobody believed that our livelihood could be improved in journeying northwards, especially with the knowledge that the jungle awaited us.

On 17th October we were taken to Singapore railway station in lorries for the start of that promised camping holiday! On arrival at the station, with thoughts perhaps of boarding some kind of passenger train, instead, with armed guards in attendance, we were ordered and herded into a goods train, a train made up of windowless steel box wagons with sliding doors on each side. Into each wagon 35 men were crammed, leaving no room for sitting or lying down, just standing room only. It was as well that we had practically no baggage. Of course, in such wagons there were no toilet facilities whatever, and this was soon to become a major problem.

We had been told that the proposed trip to our destination in Thailand would take five days, and so we departed Singapore on what was to be a most uncomfortable journey. By day those steel wagons became unbearingly hot ovens and at night the temperature within sank to the other extreme, very chilly indeed. Because of the discomfort within the wagons, during daylight hours we would take it in turns to find a space to momentarily stand near the open doors in order to get some air, and also to take in the scenery as the train rattled and swayed along through mountains and paddy fields. Although we were in captivity, and being transported like animals, there was some appreciation of the landscape as we travelled through this strange, changeable countryside of flat fields of rice paddies, banana plantations and palms, made more picturesque with a backdrop of rugged hills.

Once a day along the route northwards through Malaya, the train stopped for our meal of filthy rice and watery stew, and for the purpose of relieving ourselves. Such places as Kuala Lumpur, Ipoh and Butterworth are remembered as having bright, clean railway stations, where occasionally at these stopping places Malaysian traders took risks to secretly pass fruit to some of us. It was so obvious that the natives were in fear of the Japanese, we having already witnessed many instances of physical ill-treatment imposed upon them, so that they had to be aware of the dangers involved when trying to help us in any way, as we too needed to ensure that the guards did not detect the friendly actions by the Malays toward us.

With so many men already suffering from diarrhoea it was a great relief whenever the train stopped, although such relief was usually short-lived. The guards were constantly chasing and hurrying men along to rejoin the train, showing no pity or mercy by beating those men who were obviously in such unfit condition and so being unable to respond quickly to the guards' orders. A consequence of this meant that those afflicted with diarrhoea were often taken short whilst the train was in transit, sometimes having to be held at the open doors by their comrades to relieve themselves.

This stage of our captivity was the beginning of the degradation and suffering that we would have to endure in the future. It was also the realisation that comradeship and determination to somehow stand up to the hardships we were to encounter, would be of primary importance, if we were to pull through. Typically, there were many acts of goodwill and comradeship shown by most prisoners to their sick friends who were being violated by the Japanese guards in those instances of brutish behaviour. More often than not this ended in physical punishment for those who dared to interfere or protest against this unnecessary and outrageous treatment by the Japs. We were now well aware, as we had earlier expected, that the promised rest camp was not a reality, and we were left wondering what other disasters awaited us. But, despite all of this degradation and humiliation, the British spirit remained, and most endeavoured to make light of the circumstances with many instances of typically British Army humour.

FACE OF ADVERSITY

CHAPTER NINE

ARRIVAL AT BAM PONG – HELL CAMP NUMBER ONE

At the end of our long, wearying, five days cooped-up journey we arrived at Bam Pong, a Thai village, where we marched from the tiny station to a transit camp which had been used by other parties of P.O.Ws who had now moved further northwards. This camp in the jungle consisted of long huts built of bamboo in the like of which we were to be accommodated for the rest of our stay in Thailand. The camp area itself was an absolute quagmire; the trench latrines were overflowing due to the monsoon rains, leaving the ground a sea of black mud and sewage.

P.O.W Camp at Bam Pong, Thailand

These huts in which we were to be accommodated, standing in that filthy morass, were anything from 40 to 70 yards long, by 20 feet wide, with central gangways bounded by platforms of split bamboo some 2 feet from ground level which served as bed spaces. The gangways through which we had to walk to reach bed spaces were also ankle-deep in mud and sewage. Each hut was constructed

Interior of typical P.O.W hut at Bam Pong

of bamboo uprights with gable open ends, open sides and the roof made from Attap (dried palm fronds), the attap being tied on to narrow strips of bamboo to form tiles. It was amazing that this flimsy roofing could be rainproof at all, even during light rainfall, and of course during the heaviest of the monsoon storms which were prevalent at this time, bed spaces and any bedding soon became saturated and cold.

These hut constructions were jointed by the use of a very strong jungle growth called Rattan, which was cut into strips and used to tie the uprights to the gables - not a nail or screw was used - accommodation completely of bamboo and palm fronds. On the subject of bamboo, we were quickly to learn what a versatile growth it was. Apart from use in the building of huts, bamboo shoots were edible, and all manner and sizes of canes were used extensively by the native Thais. When cut at the joints, thick canes could be used as water carriers or as bed bottles, to which use they were later put in the jungle hospital huts.

Soon we were to see and experience a more sinister use of bamboo as applied by Japanese guards who used suitable lengths as cudgels to enforce more work from us, their slaves. Later we were also to realise the danger that the slightest scratch from contact with bamboo could cause to the human body.

Many prisoners who sustained such injuries, without the necessary medical treatment being available, often suffered horrific gangrenous tropical ulcers, which usually necessitated amputation of affected limbs in order to save lives. We were all mindful that our short spell in captivity so far had seemed fairly tough. We were not to know, nor did many of us even surmise that it could become worse than this.

FACE OF ADVERSITY

X

CHAPTER TEN

NEXT STOP CHUNGKAI – RAILWAY BUILDING, BAMBOO BASHINGS

After spending two nights at Ban Pong we travelled by trucks to a small Thai market town called Kanchanaburi some 20 miles away. Here we stayed for one night before moving on down to the river (The Kwai Noi), where we boarded barges which took us a few miles up-river to Chungkai, a Thai kampong(village). At Chungkai in a fairly large jungle clearing, were a number of huts similar to those at Ban Pong, although generally the camp here appeared a little more habitable. We learnt that Chungkai was to be the base camp for, and the commencement of our work on the Thai/Burma railway, a railway required to be built for the purpose of transportation of arms and equipment to supply Japanese forces in Burma. Thousands of prisoners were to work at, suffer at, and if death did not intervene, proceed from Chungkai northwards as the railway progressed. As the slavery, starvation, disease and illness took their toll, unfortunately too many men were never to return this way again as some of we lucky ones did on the way to freedom, albeit much later, and all with severely emaciated bodies.

So we were destined to begin our toil as jungle railway builders. The first objective set by the Japs was for us to build an embankment along a route previously cleared of jungle by earlier parties of prisoners, who had then moved on. Having settled in the camp at Chungkai, we prepared ourselves for what was to be a long, hard, tiresome task. The job was to worsen because of the sadistic and sometimes brutal actions by the Japanese engineer in charge, the English-speaking Tarumoto.

Our routine working day began early in the morning when, after a breakfast of "pap" rice, (boiled, very watery rice simulated to represent porridge, but without sweetening or milk), we paraded for roll-call when we had to line up and on the command 'bango' from the guard, we had to number in Japanese. This became another opportunity for the guards to display their hate, temper and wickedness. On failure to number correctly you could expect a tirade of abuse, and more often than not, an assault of some kind. So reluctantly, and for our own good, we began 'ichi, ni, san, si, go —' (one, two, three, four, five—).

Having thus endeavoured to start the day peacefully, and after the issue of tools for work, we would walk to the site carrying our party's food for the day in a four-gallon tin. The food, prepared and cooked overnight by our own cookhouse staff in large iron boilers called 'cwallies', consisted of the now customary boiled rice with the ever-present maggots and weevils - naturally also boiled - and referred to as our meat ration! Of course, by this time nobody considered trying to segregate and dispose of the maggots from the rice, as, with each maggot thrown out, there might also have been grains of rice attached to it. Despite the awful condition of this so-called food, nobody could ever afford to throw any of it away.

Sometimes to supplement the rice we might have a piece of sun-dried salty fish or, for a change, the cooks would send out to us a tin of what was humorously called "jungle stew", (a watery mess of boiled yam tops). Each working party also carried out with them another four-gallon tin of water, which was boiled on the site and provided the very necessary drink. Into the water was thrown a few leaves of local tea; no milk or sugar, just black, but very acceptable and essential in the heat and toil of the day.

The job of building the embankment was a boring, tedious one of digging earth and then carrying it in small wicker baskets to the site. The main implement used for digging the earth was a tool similar to a hoe, but larger, apparently of Asian origin and called a

NEXT STOP CHUNGKAI – RAILWAY BUILDING, BAMBOO BASHINGS

Preparing route of railway through Thai jungle from Chungkai into Burma

chunkel. Having hacked the earth loose with the chunkel, the baskets were then filled, carried to the site and emptied there; other members of the party spreading the earth and building up the embankment with it.

These earth-carrying baskets, which were also of Asian origin, were only five or six inches deep, about eighteen inches wide, with a handle on each side, and with capacity of only two or three shovelfuls of earth. With such small loads this meant numerous trips trudging to and from the embankment to dump the earth. Consequently, by the end of each day's work legs and bodies became very weary. Because of this, and at the instigation of the prisoners, empty rice sacks with two bamboo poles pushed through each of the corners and carried like stretchers by two men, were used to move the earth to the embankment. Obviously, more earth could be carried like this, but the method was not so monotonous as with the tiny baskets. Of course, we made sure that the volume of earth made comfortable carrying for us, but was dependant upon whether or not the guards were watching.

Normally the Japanese engineer in charge for the day would set a target for a length of embankment to be completed, and if this was achieved and was to the satisfaction of the engineer, then this system of carrying the earth on sacks could sometimes work to our advantage, allowing us to finish work earlier. There were many times of course when the Japs decided that they would prolong our working day, and it was not unusual for us to return to camp in the early hours of the next morning having worked during the hours of darkness by the light of flares. Many times on the trudge back to camp we would go straight into the river to bathe away the dirt and sweat, before retiring to our bamboo bed spaces for a short night's sleep. Often when bathing in the river, fish would nibble at the ulcers on our legs and although at first the sensation was rather disturbing, it was said that poisonous pus from the infection withdrawn by the fish in this way could possibly aid healing of the wounds. Other sensitive, tender and more personal parts of the body below the waistline also attracted the nibbling of the fishes!

During this work every opportunity was taken, when the guards were out of sight, to sabotage the construction of the embankment. This was achieved by the insertion of rotten tree trunks or any soluble articles amongst the earth deposited there instead of making it all solid fill. Similar acts were applied to the small bridges that we also erected along the railway trace. Instead of hammering home the metal spikes fully to secure the wooden spars to the

NEXT STOP CHUNGKAI – RAILWAY BUILDING, BAMBOO BASHINGS

Railway cutting through rocks at Chungkai

horizontals, many of these were left loose. The same destructive treatment was given to the metal 'dogs' which were intended to secure the rails to the sleepers, with the hope that in time to come, this too would delay the progress of the Japanese troops and supplies travelling northwards on the way to the Burma battle front.

We were well aware of the severe punishment if the guards discovered such acts of sabotage. We also knew that another result of these acts, could possibly rebound upon us and much to our detriment, as there was a distinct possibility that we would be travelling on the railway at some later date as the job progressed northwards. (As time went on we did hear of some derailments occurring, and most of us did travel on the railway we had built as we were sent up-country to continue with the line, but as far as is known, no casualties amongst prisoners.)

As well as embankment and bridge building at Chungkai, we were also engaged in rock blasting to create cuttings, with the subsequent laying of sleepers and rails through the cuttings. The blasting was achieved by boring holes in the rock face with hammer and chisel and inserting explosive charges, which the guard would then ignite. The resultant rock debris from the blastings then had to be carried in the baskets to the embankment for stabilizing the rail sleepers. Sometimes for their amusement the guard would throw an ignited charge into the river and then enjoy the achievement when fish were brought to the surface by the explosion. Needless to say, there were many occasions when some of those stunned and mutilated fish ended up back in our camp cookhouse.

On a normal working day the guard would call a halt in the job at around mid-morning for our meal, when the Japanese themselves would also have their rice and fish or vegetables. The Japanese rice always appeared more palatable than ours, being white compared with our dirty looking and maggot-infested mess. There were a few times when the senior British officer in charge of the working party would ask the Japanese officer or guard to allow a break in work for the purpose of a rest and drinks of tea. If consent was given, the guard would bellow, "Yasume" which was a Jap word we quickly learnt meant, "stop work". We occasionally used this word ourselves to appeal for a break - sometimes successfully - but more often with a retort by the guard, "Buggero, yasume ni ga" - a Japanese negative expression and curse, which we had also quickly come to understand meant, "No rest." That Japanese word "buggero" used very many times with "kura" (come here) in loud and rude terms by the guards, was a signal to us all that trouble was brewing.

Another Jap word, which we were in favour of hearing, when it was uttered by the guards, was the word "mishi" which we understood to mean, food or mealtime. Gradually we enhanced our knowledge of Japanese words, which might be advantageous to us and practised and used them when we could. There were many times when we would plead to the guards with the Jap word "benjo" which meant that we wanted to relieve ourselves. This word we often over-used simply for the purpose of "skiving" off work for a few minutes rest in the jungle, but many times this ploy was unsuccessful, the guards having eventually become wise to this and many other of our attempts at trickery.

There were a few occasions whilst working on the railway trace, when opportunities arose for some of us to buy, or otherwise obtain, duck eggs from natives who, if they were fortunate enough to get on the right side of the guards, stopped near the work place to sell their wares. These locals had learnt that prisoners wanted to know if the eggs were hard-boiled cooked, or raw, and so we and the Thais could be heard, in an amusing kind of broken pidgin English, posing the question, "Cook.? No cook.?" As well as eggs, fruit, such as pomeloes, bananas and paw paws, could also be bought; all excellent supplements for the rice meals. Although very few prisoners had money at this time because most had bartered rather than sold for cash what possessions they had, the natives were always willing to exchange their wares for items of clothing, watches or jewellery, but at this stage as far as most of us were concerned, such articles were now almost non-existent.

At Chungkai we encountered not only the Japanese engineers who were in charge of the railway project, and who themselves were not averse to outbursts of rage and acts of brutality, but also the worst of the Korean guards. These guards were responsible for the control of the prisoners whilst at work, and they dealt out punishment with beatings for anything at all, even when men had to stop work and go into the jungle to relieve themselves. These Koreans were certainly a threat to our health and safety, particularly when they considered that we were slacking off from our work. Nevertheless, we all contrived, when we thought the time was right, to 'skive off' to gain any kind of advantage, whether it be in an attempt to delay the building of the railway or to scavenge food from the Thais. In executing these risky acts it was usually a combined effort with the help of comrades watching out for the guards and giving any necessary warnings of their approach. By this time we were becoming quite adept in the art of befooling our captors, and there were always feelings of great satisfaction when we had been successful in outwitting the guards.

Occasionally we found some amusement by indicating to the guards that the war would soon be over and that they would then be building the railway, always of course, making sure that the particular guard was not too conversant with the English language. Often the Japanese would sarcastically tell us that Churchill was "number ten" and Tojo was "number one." Of course we would verbally retaliate by reversing that statement although, in these early days in captivity we were not so sure that this bold assessment of our leader impressed our captors, nor indeed did we honestly feel admiration for the man who we believed was responsible for our incarceration.

FACE OF ADVERSITY

XI

CHAPTER ELEVEN

DISEASE STRIKES, BUT A FEW CAMP IMPROVEMENTS

Here at Chungkai the Japanese engineer Tarumoto also ordered British Officers to work on the railway and despite protests from our Senior Officer, that order was carried out, the officers being given manual tasks along with the rest of us, although usually officers were kept in their own parties. It was somewhat embarrassing for most of the Other Ranks to see their own officers being forced to work, indicating that respect for rank still existed even under such conditions.

Meanwhile life went on, and as Christmas 1942 approached many prisoners were going down with tropical illnesses such as malaria, dysentery and those dreadful ulcers. Medical supplies were forever in short supply and consequently the hospital orderlies and our medical officers were hard-pressed to cope with the ever-increasing cases of sickness. The hospital hut, which was identical in structure to all the other huts, had become a place where nobody wished to go. The atmosphere there was most frightening; the physical state of the emaciated bodies of men who, a few short months earlier had been super-fit soldiers, being hard to comprehend. As well as this distressing scenario, inside and around this hut the stench emanating from the limbs of men with those gangrenous tropical ulcers was almost unbearable. It was so very hard to believe that living, human flesh could rot to such a degree.

These ulcers, as mentioned previously, usually began as simple scratches from bamboo, often sustained when hacking down poles from bamboo clumps. As the wounds developed, with no appropriate medical treatment available, the gangrenous sores ate away deeper and wider into the flesh of affected limbs until often the bones were exposed and even arteries endangered. The medical officers tried their very best to treat these cases, sometimes having to scrape the inside of the wounds with sterilised spoons, and even introducing maggots to eat away the infected flesh. It was not hard to imagine what terrible pain from those awful ulcers these brave men had to endure, and yet those of us, suffering only from dysentery and malaria, often thinking that we were very ill, but soon realising how little pain we were suffering in comparison.

In many of the serious ulcer cases where amputations were considered necessary in order to try to save life, medical officers performed miracles in having to utilise non-medical equipment, such as cookhouse carving knives and saws to carry out the required operations. Wounds were dressed with any kind of material that might be available. Sometimes the fine, soft cotton-like material from kapok trees, which grew in the area, was ideal padding for ulcers, but when this was not available even pieces of sacking had to be utilised. Whatever was used for such purposes could not be disposed of and, after washing out and sterilizing, these had to be used again and again.

It was soon that deaths resulted amongst the prisoners due to the lack of the appropriate treatment for the diseases and illnesses within the camp, and ultimately the Japanese became worried about the loss of manpower for work on the railway. Already it seemed that the job was behind schedule as for a number of days we had been subjected to shouts of "speedo" accompanied by cudgel wielding from the Japanese engineers and the guards, together with some other expletives, which were obviously unsavoury Japanese oaths.

Quite often during these "speedo" times an enraged guard would grab a tool from a prisoner and in his temper would demonstrate most vigorously how the earth should be dug and placed on the embankment. It was surprising, and very amusing to us, that the furious Jap would really slog into the work for some minutes

DISEASE STRIKES, BUT A FEW CAMP IMPROVEMENTS

whilst we stood by watching him perform. It was not long before we all slowed down and tried to get the guards to do some of our work for us, but always endeavouring to be selective as to which guard we tried it on with, and always giving encouragement by saying, "Nippon number one." This ploy sometimes worked, but never for very long.

After our officers conferred with the Japanese officer in charge we were promised better food and some medical supplies. As a result, eventually a scraggy bullock was brought to the camp and this was slaughtered by our own cookhouse workers. I recall that the poor animal was tied with a rope around its neck close up to the trunk of a tree, whereupon one of our cooks produced a hefty sledgehammer with which he struck the beast between the eyes with a vigorous blow. The bullock would shake its head and so it was hit again, this time mercifully succumbing, to be taken to the cookhouse, carved up, cooked, and distributed, mainly to the hospital patients and then to the rest of us. Some time later, some pigs were also brought to the camp and these too were slaughtered, providing much needed addition to our diets. We were then able to partake of greasy pork 'jungle' stew for as long as the fatty meat lasted.

Not only was the meat from these animals used as food, but also, after slaughter, blood was drawn off. On one occasion a number of us drank some of the blood, but most of it was preserved and allowed to set, then to be eaten as black pudding. Personally, I had none of the black pudding, and surprisingly, even in those hard times, I never fancied it as something to eat. Most of this dried blood concoction was of obvious benefit in the hospital hut for the very sick.

So time moved slowly on, and eventually the Japanese decided to issue their own form of money and decreed that working prisoners would be paid 10 cents a day, at the same time stipulating that the non-working sick would not get paid. As we now had purchasing power we were able to buy such luxuries as bananas, paw paws and eggs from natives who were allowed to come with their wares to the camp perimeter. One banana speciality which the Thais provided was the peeled fruit, sliced lengthways down the middle, sometimes dipped in batter, and fried in a pan similar to today's 'wok'. Another favourite sweet which was available was a type of fudge made from a sugary substance called 'ghula malacca', cooked with peanuts and allowed to set.

On the subject of Thai jungle food, we had become used to the custom of the natives squatting by their baskets of produce, forever chewing betel nuts and leaves, ejecting the red spittle and juice on the ground in front of them and close to the wares they were displaying. Although this was a sickly and far from pretty sight, it did not deter us from eating the food they were providing. After all, we could not afford to be too fussy about what we ate in these early days of near starvation, so long as we remained aware of, and took precautions against eating food that might be contaminated with disease. It was here at Chungkai when work finished early, that little groups of men would muster outside the huts, light small fires and cook whatever could be found that might pass as food.

Often in the surrounding fields and in parts of the jungle, wild growths of yams could be found, and these, not forgetting the green tops of these sweet vegetables also, when boiled in tin cans on the smoky fires helped to alleviate some of the hunger pains. It was here too, that most of us became aware for the first time that peanuts grew underground, being the fruit of rather small green-topped plants. Another supplement to the overall hunger of some of the prisoners was the roasting of snakes, caught and killed and then cooked in the camp fires. Lizards too provided small and very tasty pieces of white meat, after being baked in the hot ashes of the fires.

Fortunately, there was some comfort for the smokers in the camp, with tobacco in various forms, being purchased from the Thai traders. Sometimes it would be sold as whole loose leaves, being also available in shredded packs. In whatever form, and because it had such a strong flavour, most of those who bought it washed it in boiling water or, if some sugar was available, treated it with sweet water and then hung it or laid it out in the sun to dry and mature.

At one stage during these early days at Chungkai cartons of cigarette papers were available, but there came the time when only

DISEASE STRIKES, BUT A FEW CAMP IMPROVEMENTS

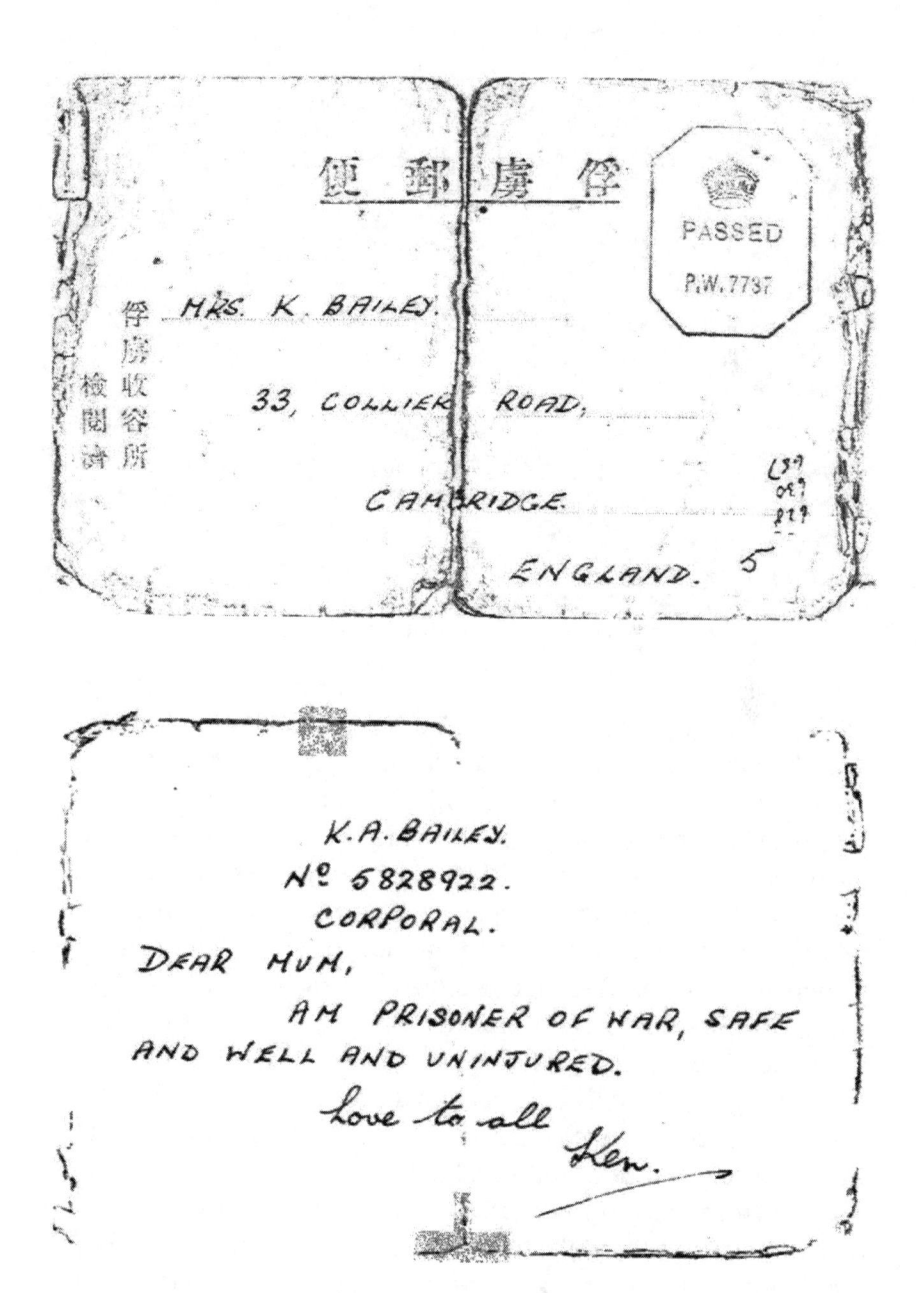

俘虜郵便

俘虜収容所
検閲済

PASSED
P.W. 7737

MRS. K. BAILEY.

33, COLLIER ROAD,

CAMBRIDGE.

ENGLAND.

K. A. BAILEY.
N° 5828922.
CORPORAL.

DEAR MUM,

AM PRISONER OF WAR, SAFE AND WELL AND UNINJURED.

Love to all

Ken.

Copy of postcard issued by the Japs to notify my family that I was a P.O.W in Thailand

> **IMPERIAL JAPANESE ARMY**
>
> I am interned in *THAILAND*
> My health is excellent.
> ~~I am ill in hospital.~~
> I am working for pay.
> ~~I am not working.~~
> Please see that *ALL AT HOME* is taken care
>
> My love to you

Copy of postcard issued by Japs notifying family as to health

course paper and leaves from the trees were the only means of having a "roll-up". As there was a shortage of matches with which to light cigarettes, in every jungle hut a small tin, containing usually some palm oil, with an ignited piece of thin rope protruding from it, served as a permanent means of a communal slow-burning cigarette lighter. This tin, with its smouldering contraption, was usually tied to a bamboo upright above bed spaces and strategically placed in the centre of the hut for the convenience of the smokers. These slow-burning rope 'fag' lighters - and most huts furnished a number of them - could smoulder for hours, serving also as a deterrent to the presence of mosquitoes.

As thoughts of Christmas occupied our minds we were told by the Japanese that we would be granted a day off on Christmas Day, although very few of us put much faith in this promise. Normally, days off from work on the railway were only for those who were very sick and confined to the hospital hut. Generally speaking, as time went on, for the workers anyway, most lost touch as to which day of the week it was, although this first Christmas Day as prisoners of war was remembered by everyone. At about this time we

DISEASE STRIKES, BUT A FEW CAMP IMPROVEMENTS

were each given a pre-printed postcard to complete for sending to our families, and although this seemed to give us some little hope that perhaps there might be contact with the outside world, we still had doubts whether the cards would reach their destinations thousands of miles away.

The introduction of wages for the workers meant that those men in the hospital huts would especially benefit as a proportion of those wages was deducted to provide the means to purchase any requirements in the hospitals. At the same time, the Japanese permitted our officers to borrow money by way of some form of credit; some of this money also being used to provide a little extra food for the hospital. Although this money was a bonus, it helped only a little towards the purchase of medicines which still remained in very short supply.

CHAPTER TWELVE

OUTSIDE HELP WITH FOOD AND MEDICAL SUPPLIES

At this time we were hearing stories that a Thai businessman had made contact with the British officers and was organizing facilities to provide food and also some medical supplies for our camp. It was also known that the Japanese had given permission for one of our officers, accompanied by a Jap guard, to visit Kanchanburi, the market town and location of our previous camp, and there to purchase some provisions for Chungkai camp. There seemed to be no doubt that Kanchanburi was the contact place of the officer and the Thai benefactor, later to be known as a Mr. Boonpong.

This was a worrying time, not only for the prisoners, but also it seemed, for the Japanese. Much concern was being shown regarding the daily increase in sickness within the camp; the Japanese still being particularly uneasy about depleted working parties for railway work as well as fear of contraction of disease themselves.

At one point, because of the incidence of dysentery within the camp, it was suggested by the Japanese that we should arm ourselves with any form of flycatcher, catch as many flies as possible, and for every man who caught 30 flies, a reward of a rice rissole would be given by the camp cookhouse. We all of course jumped at the chance for extra food and proceeded to swat as many flies as possible with whatever means, at the same time being conscious of the obvious benefits to our health in destroying the carriers of that awful disease, as well as satisfying our hunger with the additional rice rissoles.

Flies became such a hazard mainly because most of us by this time were suffering from dysentery. Since those who suffered could seldom control themselves in endeavouring to get to the latrines, the camp area became contaminated, so attracting the disease-carrying insects. Apart from this, the latrines in most camps were usually overflowing due to heavy rains, and this naturally exacerbated the dysentery situation. Of all the tropical diseases suffered by the prisoners at this time, dysentery in particular was most depressing. Apart from the obvious urgency when stomach pains occurred, and the added embarrassment of failing to reach the latrines in time, there was no such luxury as toilet paper or of any other kind of paper. It was a case of finding anything that could be used for the purpose in the undergrowth, or leaves from trees, (but never banana fronds which always split laterally under pressure, with obvious results!)

Those of us who suffered from this debilitating disease dysentery, were forever making visits to those awful latrines. These foul, disgusting places throughout the camps in Thailand were all the same, just long trenches dug in the ground within each camp, with bamboo poles laid across the width of the trenches on which the users had to stand and squat over those filthy pits. There was no privacy, no separate cubicle, and more often than not, without cover overhead. Just a line of squatting bodies out in the open, racked with intense pain, suffering also the irritation caused by millions of flies and mosquitoes buzzing around, as well as drenching rain, or scorching heat from the sun on unprotected bodies.

Of course whilst flies were the greatest spreaders of disease, everyone suffered too with much discomfort from lice, which caused persistent itching. But worse than lice was the permanent presence of bed bugs. These horrible brown, foul-smelling, detestable insects made their homes in the slit bamboo of our bed spaces drawing blood from the human body, and when we destroyed them the air became full of the smell of rotten almonds. This obnoxious odour was particularly abhorrent at night, and that, together with the continual nuisance of mosquitoes biting and buzzing around, as well as those irritable lice, caused many sleepless hours.

OUTSIDE HELP WITH FOOD AND MEDICAL SUPPLIES

By now we had become accustomed to other jungle creatures, all of which we considered could cause us much discomfort if we were not careful. Such as scorpions and centipedes could give one a nasty nip, whilst spiders, as large as a human hand, and brown and furry, were not favourite bed partners. These were creatures with which we had close contact, and which we could quite easily dispose of, but there were also others which showed themselves from time to time. We were continually aware of the danger from snakes, but only on two occasions did I catch sight of any of these slimy, fearsome creatures, both being in the open jungle. As far as I can recall there were no instances when these reptiles were found inside the camp huts.

At times we also saw elephants at close quarters when they were used to move heavy timber from the jungle to the railway embankment. A story existed that the Japanese decided that after a time these animals were far too slow for that particular job, and so they were dismissed in favour of the prisoners, who then had to manually move the tree trunks to the railway site. There were also other jungle creatures we became aware of, often hearing the echoing chatter of monkeys at night, and the shrill night calls of various birds. On some occasions whilst working on the railway trace we would watch jungle fowl with their brightly coloured plumage, which very much resembled pheasants. These instances, together with quite picturesque views of rugged mountains, brought some brightness into the dull, generally unhealthy climate of the monsoon jungle.

By now clothing, and footwear too, had long been worn out and so improvisation had to come to the fore. At work we were all exposed to the sun; those with unprotected bodies, including the feet, now having the appearance somewhat of the native Thais. It was very unfortunate for the fair to red-haired prisoners, who of course suffered much discomfort from the effects of that burning sun. So everyone was always on the lookout, especially for anything that could be utilised to cover the feet as well as the body. Such things as pieces of rubber from any old vehicle tyres, or suitable wood which could be fashioned into clogs, flip-flops or sandals were priceless as far as foot comfort was concerned, although such flimsy foot covering gave little protection from bamboo injury when working on the railway trace, and this was a danger of which we all had to be aware if we did not want to end up with those dreaded ulcers.

As for wearing apparel, any rice sacks or parts of them were useful for this purpose, often being utilised as bodily protection against the powerful heat of the tropical sun. Also, a rice sack became a fairly common bed blanket. However, for those who were prone to malarial relapses, a sack would give little comfort when the sufferer was lying on his uncomfortable split bamboo bed space in the throes of cold, shivering sweats. In such instances, one would often find that a colleague was willing to give up his own bed cover, whether it be a blanket or rice sack, in order to afford some extra warmth and comfort to his friend.

Even if one was fortunate enough to possess covering of any kind - blankets or rice sacks - what comfort these provided in terms of warmth was spoilt by the presence always of those irritable lice. These parasites made their homes in anything that the human body made contact with, finding their way into seams or turn-ups of any clothing and sacking too, becoming most irritable. Prisoners could always be seen sitting on their beds, or wherever else they might be, cracking the lice between their thumbs. But this was a never-ending task and it was only by steeping affected clothing, blankets or sacks, in boiling water that any short relief was achieved, with irritation soon returning.

The subject of lice reminds me of two or three instances earlier when we were travelling by lorries accompanied as usual by Jap guards. One guard used to stand in the front of the lorry facing forwards with us standing behind him, the other guard standing in the rear. I decided that the guard in front of me might like to share some lice, which were irritating me around the waistband of my ragged shorts. As I was very close to him it was easy for me to transfer some of these pests on to his clothing without being seen either by him or his fellow guard at the rear. In doing this I hoped that the lice would cause the guard as much discomfort as they had to me, and soon everyone was doing his best to share the lice with our captors. It was little things like this that gave us some satisfaction and amusement without too much risk of being caught in the act and suffering the consequences.

Although at most of the railway camps we were not fenced in, escape was never a real option. It had been obvious from the outset that any attempt at escape from the jungle was ill-advised and almost impossible. Surrounding the camps was a dense, tangled mass of jungle trees and vegetation. Survival from any endeavour to escape in such conditions would depend, not only on being able to find the way westwards to the sea, there being no hope of escape by land, but also the availability of food. There would also be danger from animals and disease, as well as the possibility of meeting up with unfriendly, pro-Japanese natives and betrayal by them.

FACE OF ADVERSITY

XIII

CHAPTER THIRTEEN

ESCAPE NO OPTION – ENVIRONMENT UNFRIENDLY

It was here at Chungkai that we heard of two prisoners, believed Australians, who had been caught trying to escape from one of the camps nearby. On capture they had been made to dig a trench, forced to kneel by the edge of it, then they were shot dead so that they fell into the trench. There were also similar stories when escapes were attempted, only to fail, and the unfortunate captives meeting a worse death by decapitation.

In addition to the sufferings caused by dysentery, beriberi, malaria and tropical ulcers, lack of decent food naturally meant vitamin deficiency. This resulted in other painful and distressing complaints, such as sore and itching scrotums, sore tongues and disease of the skin, including many cases of ringworm and jaundice also. More seriously was the disturbing effect that lack of vitamins had caused to many men whose sight had become impaired. But still the ceaseless, compelling forced labour had to go on with everybody striving to fight weariness and sickness as well as the seemingly perpetual threat of atrocious behaviour by the Jap guards for the slightest reasons.

Deaths amongst the prisoners were beginning to occur daily, with burial days being terribly sad and mournful occasions. More often than not the burials were attended only by the Army Chaplain and, where one existed, the camp bugler, but unfortunately very few other prisoners, due to work enforcement. Despite the appalling conditions in which we were existing here, every effort was made by British officers to insist that the Japanese allow our dead to be given dignified and respectable burials, and generally they complied with those requests without imposition of any kind of restrictions, apart from the necessity that the railway work still had to proceed.

The burial ground at Chungkai was a clearing at the rear of the camp, which to this day is the site of Chungkai War Graves Commission Cemetery, a well-administered and beautifully maintained memorial to those who died as prisoners so far from home. On such depressing occasions when comrades died under these dreadful and evil circumstances the thoughts of us all wondered and questioned whether civilization existed at all. However, from time to time whilst working on the railway trace we would see Buddhist monks dressed in saffron coloured robes, usually two or three walking in single file along the jungle track, giving us just the merest glance, never speaking, but eye contact with us was sufficient to show that we were in their thoughts. It was obvious that these religious people were very much afraid of the Japanese and so refrained from any other contact with us. We felt that these were indications that decency and Christianity were existing somewhere nearby despite the wickedness which was being imposed upon us daily by our captors.

Despite the rapid incidence of the number of prisoners suffering illness and the increase in deaths, the Japanese insisted that the building of the railway had to proceed. They threatened that food supplies would be cut if many prisoners were certified by the doctors as being too sick to leave the camp to work. As a result, many of us who were suffering from malaria and dysentery had to make the numbers up for work parties, these illnesses not considered by the Japanese to be serious enough for hospitalisation. There were no signs that an increase in medical supplies was forthcoming, only small and infrequent doses of powdered quinine being available for the worst cases of malaria.

If one had dysentery, treatment was practically nil. The only thing I can recall being prescribed for this disease was to eat charcoal and drink water, the charcoal being obtained from wood fires in the camp and water from the adjacent river, which of course had to be made sterile by boiling. Anyone suffering from dysentery got very little relief from such treatment and so, whether in camp or at work, these were very traumatic and depressing times for those men.

In spite of the appalling physical condition of the prisoners and the many deaths then occurring in the camp, the Japanese still continued with cruel and bestial treatment towards some of their captives. As well as beatings with bamboo poles, one method of punishment which seemed to give them weird, sadistic satisfaction was to stand the alleged offender to attention in the sun, bareheaded and holding a large boulder or other heavy object above his head, with the threat of a swipe from a bamboo cudgel if any movement was made. This was a common scenario at Chungkai and one of the many ways of Japanese uncivil administration and ruthless control of discipline! As well as witnessing all these sadistic acts at Chungkai, we were constantly hearing horrendous stories of ill-treatment from other camps, such as the Japanese water punishment in which an offending prisoner would be forced to drink water until he could drink no more when he would be laid down and have his stomach repeatedly jumped upon by the guards.

Although life was not without incidents which were alien to us, and being well aware of the dangers of upsetting our captors - at which times some kind of punishment always resulted - everyone had to endeavour to look on the bright side whenever possible. This of course was not possible for those who were lying in the hospital hut knowing that the doctors could do very little to help them in recovery. Men who were reasonably fit, including officers, tried their very best to make camp life easier by organising such events as musical evenings and stage shows. With permission of the Japanese of course, an area in the camp was set aside for those prisoners who had the aptitude for entertaining, and although these performances occurred very rarely, the intentions of the organisers were commendable. These occasions were usually arranged for a day which was called a Japanese rest day, when sometimes we were given a day off from work. Such days were few and far between, and most men, when they had any chance of respite from forced labour took such opportunity to endeavour to get some rest on those uncomfortable bamboo bed spaces. The musical side of such evenings usually took the form of a low-spirited singsong by those attending.

XIV

CHAPTER FOURTEEN

NORTHWARDS TO CHOLERA AND BERI-BERI AT HELL CAMP NUMBER TWO

When our job was completed at Chungkai we moved on, sometimes marching and sometimes travelling on the railway trucks northwards to other camps such as Wampo, Tarsao, Kinsayok and finally Martona. Such journeys were always a hard slog and although many of us were now getting used to the intense heat of the tropical sun, and the rigours of suffering foot weariness, there was nothing new that we could look forward to when moving to another camp. At the end of each journey the next jungle camp resembled, or was more primitive than, the previous one, with illness and disease just as rife, and food and medical supplies shorter than ever.

It was at Tarsao camp that I met my brother-in-law Jack Spivey from Cambridge. He was a Quartermaster in the Royal Engineers, but it was only a brief meeting before our party was moving on again towards Martona Camp, which was to be our final stay in the north. Jack sadly died while a captive on 30th May 1943 age 30 years. He is buried at Thanbyuzayat War Cemetery.

This part of our journey northwards was mainly on foot, the rest being by train along the recently laid track, which, at Wampo, traversed a viaduct by way of a bridge, built on tall piles sunk in a riverbed around the side of a steep rock face. Travelling the very acute bend around the rock was most precarious, with the train of open trucks in which we were packed, slowly screeching its way along, everyone in fear that derailment would send us all down into the river bed below. There was a point where the train came to a standstill because of the acuteness of the bend and we all had to de-truck and bodily ease the train along whilst ensuring that we kept our feet firmly on the sleepers or rails. One false step or slip could have meant plunging from the track into the rocky river bed some hundred feet below.

Arriving at Martona we found it to be a small camp bearing no comparison with the others, being merely a messy clearing in the jungle in which were pitched a few bell tents, these to serve as our only shelter. It was at this camp that we first became aware of the existence of cholera, a most frightening disease apparently borne along in the adjacent swollen river and spreading quickly. The increasing extent of this disease was said to have been due to the unhygienic habits of Indian Tamils, who were also forced to work for the Japanese, and who, it was said, used to perform all their toilet motions in the river.

Every camp along the route of the railway was close to the river and each relied on the river water for drinking, washing and eating and so, more than ever before, the boiling of water and the sterilisation of eating utensils was absolutely essential. For these purposes, in all camps a large container of boiling water was always provided, mainly in the vicinity of each cookhouse, into which all utensils had to be dipped before drinking or eating from them.

Those who contracted cholera had no chance of survival, it was sudden and awful, changing a man in a matter of hours from an ordinary, reasonably fit person to a thin skeleton from head to toes, with eyes sunken and rolling. Of course at this Martona camp those men with cholera were isolated and tended in a hospital tent away from the rest of us. Each day we heard of at least one death from this disease and each day sick parades revealed more possible cholera cases. I saw men pitifully standing in the sick parade queue being aware that they had the symptoms, and knowing that the medical officers could do very little for them. This was a most distressing time and those men who were fairly fit felt so helpless in being unable to give comfort to those unfortunate and very sick comrades. It seemed that the only treatment for cholera cases was by way of saline, but apparently this treatment was effective only if given intravenously, and the Japanese had not supplied the necessary equipment for this purpose.

Our medical officers at Martona camp were so burdened in trying to cope with the sick load so a few of the fairly fit men - two close friends of mine were such persons - volunteered to assist in the cholera tent. These were acts of bravery indeed, and I'm pleased to say that both pals survived, to return home in 1945. Naturally at this disease-ridden camp we were all well aware about the risks of catching cholera and so the precaution of sterilising eating and drinking utensils was rigidly adhered to, nobody daring to be neglectful of carrying out this simple and necessary action. It was serious enough that we were all suffering from one or more of the other diseases that were rife at that time, without inviting cholera.

As far as I was concerned my own health was at a low ebb at this time, malaria and dysentery being ever-present, and also beriberi had taken a firm hold. Beriberi was a deficiency disease brought on by malnutrition, and of the two types- 'wet' and 'dry' -I suffered the former. This caused gross enlargement of the limbs, in my case the legs, which became really fat and bloated from the ankles up to my knees. When pressure was applied to the flesh, deep indentations resulted and remained so for some minutes. I likened this effect to that of bladders of lard seen in butchers' shops back in England, on which, when finger pressure was applied, the dented impressions remained for some time afterwards.

The most frightening aspect of 'wet' beriberi was, that the higher the swelling moved up the body towards the chest and heart, then the outcome could be serious. It was said that once the heart was affected then chance of recovery became very slim. In many cases of this disease, private parts became grossly swollen and most painful. This was a really scary time for all of us suffering from a disease that most had never heard of before. The 'dry' beriberi category was no less serious than the other; the main symptoms of this being the opposite, in that limbs became very thin and skin discoloured. With both cases of beriberi there was also severe aching of the whole of the body, accompanied by extreme tiredness. The only additional means of treatment for beriberi was polished rice, purported to contain vitamins that would help to supply the nutrition we all needed, and especially for those of us suffering from deficiency illnesses such as beriberi. Needless to say, very little of this rice nor any other treatment was forthcoming.

There were at this time so many of us who were too sick to work regularly that the Japs, so concerned about their own health, and still fearful of being struck down with disease themselves, ordered that the very sick prisoners, but not the cholera cases, would be evacuated down-country, leaving only reasonably fit men to carry on with the railway work and some others helping in the cholera tent. Although still able to work, but suffering dysentery, malaria and beriberi, luckily I was one of a dozen or so other men, selected to be evacuated.

FACE OF ADVERSITY

XV

CHAPTER FIFTEEN

EVACUATION SOUTHWARDS TO RUMOURS, COFFEE AND FOOTBALL!

When the day and the hour arrived for us to leave this horror camp, we set off on foot moving as quickly as our legs would take us, heading towards the river where we were to board barges for our trip South. As we strode out I remember my pal Dennis Moore frantically saying, "Step on it before they change their minds." We certainly hurried along that jungle track as well as our bloated, tired legs would enable us so to do, being in no mind to stay at this hell camp Martona, and feeling sure that by moving back down-country we had to have a much better chance of survival. Arriving at the river and having embarked, the barges moved us down river slowly and onward back towards the base camp Chungkai, from where we had begun our railway slavery a year before.

On arrival at Chungkai I learnt that one of my closest friends, and a great footballing goalkeeper, 'Dusty' Miller, who had been left behind in the hospital hut here when the rest of us had moved up-country, had not survived from the effects of the horrific leg ulcer for which he was receiving treatment when we had left him. When I last saw 'Dusty' he was in considerable pain from a shin wound six inches long, the flesh eaten away almost down to the shin-bone and around towards the back of his leg revealing a large, putrid cavity. Of course, without the required medical help, such serious cases seldom survived, often release from the excruciating pain and suffering coming only from death. Private William

'Dusty' Miller, 5830438 5th Suffolk Regiment, had been buried at Chungkai Cemetery on 10th October 1943.

Conditions at Chungkai Camp had changed considerably. Although the same huts were there, it appeared that the camp as a whole had been cleaned up and there was an air of reasonable organisation apparent. Food was infinitely better than before, as was the availability of some medical supplies, in particular quinine for the treatment of malaria. This, and other medicines were believed to have been a proportion of Red Cross parcels for prisoners received some months earlier, much of which had been purloined by the Japanese.

Now back at Chungkai again it was pleasing to find that no longer were there the enforced working parties that this camp provided for the building of the railway on our previous visit. Instead, the only tasks here were those within and for the general upkeep of the camp, sometimes including unloading rice etc. from the river barges, and also work in the hospital hut. Even the hospital hut conditions had improved slightly although it was still a dis-

EVACUATION SOUTHWARDS TO RUMOURS, COFFEE AND FOOTBALL!

gusting place for the care and nursing of civilized human beings whose bed spaces were still of bug-ridden split bamboo. Despite of all that which we had seen and suffered, it was soon that we who had come from up-country began to feel much fitter, although those of us still suffering from dysentery never lost the symptoms that caused continual visits to the camp latrines; and there were always periods when malarial relapses would strike with feverish shivers and sweats. Nevertheless, we who had seen the intense suffering of friends at Martona had to be grateful for the comparative relief of life at Chungkai.

Some of the resident P.O.W's at Chungkai at this time had set themselves up in the business of providing others with little food luxuries - such as there could be had in the existing austere conditions. One such group devised a way of simulating a coffee drink, this being achieved by roasting grains of rice, boiling this charred mass in a 4 gallon tin of water, adding some acquired sugar and selling the black, liquid mixture at 10cents a cup. Others opened up a marmalade-making business by collecting limes, which grew plentifully in the area, adding sugar and selling the resultant concoction. Although toast was not on our menu, there being no bread available, the boiled rice tasted considerably more appetizing with a touch of lime marmalade. Another change at Chungkai was the efforts made by prisoners to grow vegetables, such as sweet potatoes, beans and spinach. Wherever possible, small sections of soil had been cultivated in order to raise such crops, so providing, not just the essential extra food, but also a means of occupational therapy.

After a short and quite pleasant respite at Chungkai we were on the move again southwards, travelling by train, this time for a brief spell at Non Pladuk, one of two camps adjacent to railway sidings and workshops. Here we worked within the railway buildings, but we were not under the pressure that we had experienced up-country, and in general, life was much more civilized. Accommodation was in fairly substantial wooden huts with more reasonable toilet facilities than before, and some of us had even become fit enough to play in a football match organised by one of the Korean guards. This man was a decent sort as Koreans go, one who was well-versed in the English language, believed to be slightly Americanised and so nick-named "The Yank". This Korean, unlike any others we had encountered, was popular with us all because, not only did he speak our language, but seemed to be genuinely interested in the welfare of the prisoners.

One game of football "The Yank" arranged was between a team of prisoners, in which I played, against a mixed team of Japanese and Koreans. Most of the P.O.W's and also some visiting Jap officers watched this game. Unfortunately, just when we were beginning to enjoy the confrontation, leading by a number of goals, some rough play developed, perpetrated I have to admit by we British. Because of this, the Jap officers ordered that the game be abandoned. There were a few signs, and this action by the Jap officers in having the football match abandoned, and the fact that we were showing aggression towards our captors on the field of play, indicated that times were changing. This attitude was very much due to the fact that we were now constantly hearing rumours that the Japanese were losing the war in the Pacific, and we began to surmise that the friendliness of "The Yank" may have been a consequence of this.

FACE OF ADVERSITY

XVI

CHAPTER SIXTEEN

SAILING AGAIN – RETURN TO SINGAPORE BUT NO LUXURY TRIP!

Soon orders were issued that all fit prisoners were to be taken to Japan, and so Japanese and British medical officers arranged sick parades to determine which men would be in good enough condition to make such a journey. It was on such a sick parade that I discovered that I weighed just a shade over 9 stones, my weight having been 12 stones on arrival at Singapore. I cannot recall being too disturbed about my loss of weight, although for the first time in years, I saw myself in a fairly full length mirror and I was shocked by the reflection of my skinny torso. My fat beriberi legs were slowly beginning to get back to normality, and I suppose that my feelings at this time were that I was fortunate to be still surviving and being able to play football, despite being just a lightweight with podgy legs.

Before categorization of prisoners for sending to Japan we all had to line up outside our huts for the purpose of a rectal medical examination. This, we were told, was to ensure that no carriers of the cholera disease would be sent to Japan. This examination necessitated each of us to remove our shorts, bend down in front of a Jap medical orderly who then inserted a glass pipette into our rear. Not a pleasant operation out in the open and in the blazing hot sun; nor did it present a pretty sight.

Eventually a large party, including myself, and fortunately a few of my own battalion, left Non Pladuk by rail on a journey back to

Singapore, where on arrival we went to River Valley camp, a camp housing British, Australian and Dutch prisoners. From here we went daily in groups to Singapore where we worked on the docks, sometimes loading or unloading ships and also doing jobs within the warehouses. At this time most of us were feeling very much fitter, but not ecstatic about the prospect of going to Japan. Nevertheless, every move away from the Thailand jungle gave us a little more hope of survival with the possibility of being free from those indecent, open huts and disease-ridden latrines.

The food situation here at River Valley was reasonable. The staple diet was still rice, but now prepared and cooked in various ways. Christmas 1944 was spent at this camp, and by now the cookhouse workers were quite proficient at preparing food to at least appear more appetising, even experimenting with variations of boiled, fried and ground rice, the latter being utilised as flour from which the cooks produced baked bread and cakes,(of sorts). There were also some meals, which were accompanied by small portions of unnamed meat. We were not put off by the fact that there was talk that some Australian prisoners had been seen killing dogs which had ventured into the camp area. We had long ago reached the stage of not asking questions, nor caring too much about the food we were given, except to know that whatever we ate or drank was safe, so long as we could be sure that it had been thoroughly cooked or boiled.

After five or six days spent at River Valley camp we were transported to Singapore Docks where we boarded a small, dirty, rusty old merchant ship of Dutch origin, the "Fuij Nord" built in 1909, tonnage 3,500. The 2,500 or so prisoners were forced into the hold of the ship until it became full. A few of us, not relishing the thought of spending time below decks in those crowded, uncomfortable conditions, luckily, but more likely by surreptitious means, found space on deck amongst bits of heavy cargo. Here on the top deck and in the open, we considered that if any disaster befell the ship during our journey we might well stand a better chance of survival.

Eventually the ship moved out of Singapore heading East and

SAILING AGAIN – RETURN TO SINGAPORE BUT NO LUXURY TRIP!

then North, most of us still under the impression that our destination was Japan. Conditions on board were atrocious. We saw that our rice, which was not the off-white kind we had been used to hitherto, was a dark brown colour full of rice husks - we were told that the husks would provide us with the vitamins we so badly needed! Our meals were prepared and then cooked in large iron boilers, which were situated on the open deck. I well remember that often during mealtimes our food was impregnated with smuts from the ship's funnel; it really was amazing what one could stomach when hungry, but by this time we had all become men with insatiable hunger for food of any kind, and in whatever condition.

The toilet facilities on board were not much better than those we had experienced in the jungle. Washing with salt water took place on deck by way of a hosepipe, and as for usage of latrines, well this was certainly different, perhaps one could even say, dangerously thrilling. These so-called latrines consisted of large wooden crates; having had part of the bottoms removed leaving an open space in the centre. The crates were hung over and outside the ship's rails and lashed to the rails with ropes, leaving the whole contraption suspended over the sea. To use a latrine it was necessary for one to climb over the rails, lowering oneself into the crate, squatting down whilst making sure that the feet were either side of the space in the centre. To be able to get into such position was a feat in itself, and then having to keep an eye on the ocean below as well as on the ship's rail where a firm hand grip was needed to ensure stability and safety.

I hope that this description of the suspended high-rise, mid-air latrine- P.O.W. style - needs no further explanation. I'm pleased to say that to my knowledge no P.O.W. was lost at sea on this particular trip by falling through or out of such a latrine, but to use it was precarious indeed, and not a little frightening as we were well aware that the journey was taking us through shark-infested seas!

On the second night out from Singapore whilst being escorted by other small ships, at 11pm our ship was rocked as a terrific explosion was heard. It seemed that a missile had hit our ship, and then there were further explosions. Those of us who were on deck saw that one of the escorting ships was sinking fast in the darkness, and it soon became apparent that our ship was still afloat and obviously had not been hit. No doubt the attack on the sinking ship by torpedo or depth charges perhaps was the reason why we at first thought we had been attacked. So we sailed on through the night, everyone, including the Japs, apprehensive about the rest of the journey. Those of us on deck gradually dropped into uneasy sleep. Without doubt the unfortunate men within the ship's holds found no appeasement in their overcrowded conditions, and had much less sleep than we. In comparison, at least on deck in the open we felt some degree of safety, as well as comfort from the sea breezes.

Suddenly at 5am the next morning we experienced an almost identical happening as had occurred six hours earlier; again there were explosions and the ship shook and rocked as before, but remained unscathed. When dawn broke our ship was the only one in sight, those that had comprised our convoy when we had set sail having disappeared. Thankfully, our ship was the only one of the convoy carrying prisoners. The Japanese told us that those ships, which had disappeared during the night, had been sunk by submarines, and this news encouraged us to believe that our days as prisoners were drawing to a close.

XVII

CHAPTER SEVENTEEN

INDO-CHINA – MORE HARD WORK, BUT GOOD NEWS TOO

Later that day, 8th February 1945, our ship docked at Saigon, Indo-China where we were very relieved to disembark and to be later accommodated in dockside buildings. There were signs here of bomb damage as we saw a number of half-sunken ships lying in the harbour and also some damaged buildings in the vicinity. At the time of our arrival we were given a great boost when we were told that American 'planes had flown over the docks area shortly before, but no bombs had been dropped. For this we were grateful after our frightening experiences at sea hours earlier although happy that our allies were operating in the area.

After a few days working around the dock area and also at Saigon airfield, a party of us were marched along the South East coast of Indo-China finally arriving at the small town of Da Lat. This was a neat European/French-influenced town consisting of brick-built tiled houses the like of which we had not seen since leaving Singapore months earlier. We eventually arrived at a compound of half a dozen substantially built buildings situated on the outskirts of Da Lat and here we were to encamp for only a few days. The weather in this area was quite different to the humidity we had experienced before. The temperature was low and the absence of the sun was so noticeable. We were thankful that the huts, which we now occupied, were not built of bamboo and open to the elements as were the huts in the Thailand jungle. In the open centre of the camp area was situated a brick-built communal bath into which we put buckets of hot water obtained from the cookhouse and where we all enjoyed the first hot baths since our arrival at Singapore three years before.

The work we were set to carry out here was that of the continuation of the construction of an underground war bunker for the Japanese. Our particular task was to dig and remove earth from the coal-mine type face at the end of a tunnel which had been excavated through a large grass-covered hill. The tunnel was laid with a rail track, together with trucks for removing the earth from the face to the exit. This job was not very popular except for those few who had experienced work in coal-mines, but for those of us who had not been underground before, it was a little frightening. Thankfully the job was to last for just two days.

The spirit of each of us at this time was noticeably changing for the better, particularly with the news that allied submarines were active in the area. For some months the feelings had been, that apart from rumours of successes by the Allied forces in the Pacific area, there were also signs that the Japanese guards generally, were becoming slightly more sociable towards us. This did not however seem to be the case when, one night when most of us were sleeping, we were roused from our beds by a guard. A Japanese officer who was obviously under the influence of drink accompanied this guard, and we were ordered to stand by our beds for inspection.

There we all were, standing to attention in various states of undress, most without any clothing at all, and the officer, having drawn his sword, walked along and in front of us, selecting one or two of those who were naked to place the tip of the sword under the men's private parts. This was highly amusing for the guards and the officer, but there were no signs of jollity on our faces. No harm came to anyone however, but for a few minutes there was naturally some anxiety felt by all of us, especially as the officer was very drunk. Apart from this incident our aspirations were definitely in the ascendancy for, on a number of occasions we had heard the sounds of aircraft high overhead and we hoped and believed that these might have been Allied war 'planes on missions against the Japanese.

After the underground job was completed our party moved back towards Saigon where we were to be employed on maintenance of

INDO-CHINA – MORE HARD WORK, BUT GOOD NEWS TOO

the railway track close to a busy siding. It was here whilst working on the track one morning that the Japanese Corporal in charge of us screamed at us to run into the jungle as an aircraft was coming. We left the track at speed to take cover in the trees and prepared to await the arrival of the aircraft. Meanwhile our corporal guard, who was rather corpulent and not built for speed, was well behind us, running from the railway embankment, screaming as he ran, creating the amusing picture of being chased by the 'plane which we could then hear approaching. We saw the guard throw his rifle into a trench by the track and he quickly followed until he was lost from our sight.

FACE OF ADVERSITY

XVIII

CHAPTER EIGHTEEN

AMERICAN AIRCRAFT AND FREEDOM AT LAST

We were all still enjoying the incident when an aircraft appeared from our left flying very low and following the railway line. We had a wonderful view from the edge of the jungle less than a hundred yards away of an American Lockheed Hudson bomber, so close that we could see the occupant of its gun turret as it went by. This was of course, a most exciting and thrilling incident, which gave us a tremendous fillip. Within minutes there was an enormous chain of explosions as the aircraft reached and passed the sidings some distance to our right. We learnt afterwards that an ammunitions train had been destroyed and we now knew that our friends and allies must be moving closer toward us.

Our small party of around twenty men was then moved to a hut in a jungle clearing close to the Saigon railway track and some miles from Saigon itself. I was put in charge of this party and the Jap guard was the same corporal who had panicked when the American bomber had appeared on the previous job. At this site our task was to build a small bridge for the purpose of taking the railway track from a nearby siding. This first of all entailed carrying hefty tree trunks from the jungle. To do this the trunks were manhandled by the prisoners to the site by means of wooden poles placed under the trunks with the men in pairs on opposite sides of the trunks, lifting in unison and carrying them step by step. Bearing in mind the great weight of the trees it was necessary that the six to eight men who were doing the carrying had to be given a signal by me for the simultaneous picking up and placing down of the trees.

With knowledge that our friends and allies were now close at hand and confident that the war would soon be over, I gave frequent signals for the men to lower the trees to enable them to have as many rests from carrying as was possible. It was because of such actions by me that the Japanese corporal lost his temper and cuffed me around my head bawling, "No rest, speedo." This was only minor admonishment and we carried on as before, having rests when it was felt necessary. We were no longer in fear of the guard and he allowed us to carry on in our own time. I think this was the moment when we began to anticipate that we were soon to be in charge.

It was a few days later that whilst I was directing the operations of driving in the piles for the bridge, at the time being seated on the top of a tripod above the manual pile-driver, that some Japanese officers arrived on the site. These officers called the guard to them and they all left the site and walked into the jungle. From my elevated position on the tripod it seemed that the Japs were having tense conversation and I well recall shouting down to the men below that I believed that this was a sign that the war was over. At the time I did not feel over-confident in my belief, but there was a definite feeling of hope because of recent happenings. Within a few minutes the Japanese emerged to announce to us that work was finished for the day and that we were to return to camp. Back in camp we were all agog, spirits were high and there was a certain air of expectancy amongst us, especially as we saw that the Japanese were grouped together in their hut, talking excitedly as they appeared to be engrossed in reading from papers of some sort.

That night was not a time for sleeping for many of us, most were looking forward in anticipation to some formal announcement that would favourably concern us. For myself, I certainly had a mostly sleepless night, and an uncomfortable one too because of a malarial relapse, which caused me, when sleep did come, to have nightmarish dreams that I was hauling tree trunks through the gangway of our hut. In waking from my feverish nightmare and still suffering from the effects of dysentery, I needed to visit the latrines. I was in no state to negotiate the walk from the hut by myself because of the malarial shivers and high temperature, and had to be assisted by one of my fellow prisoners. The Jap guard at the hut entrance challenged us and, on being told that I had malaria he took from his pocket a Mepacrine tablet, which he gave to me. Although we suspected that this tablet was once part of the Red Cross parcel medicines sent out for P.O.W's for treatment of malaria, but stolen by the Japs, it was gratefully accepted. I went back to bed hopefully thinking that this gesture was a sign that the Japs were losing the war, rather than that this particular Japanese benefactor was civilized after all!

The next day we were called from our hut, assembled before a Japanese officer who announced to us that the war was over and that Tokyo had been bombed. We were later told that we were to return to Saigon the next day. Although we all had plenty to converse about, I do not recall any loss of control of discipline by anyone, we were just happy and sensible enough to await developments.

Early the next day we were picked up by a train which took us to Saigon, and then we were transported by lorry to a former French Indo-China barracks on the outskirts of Saigon City. Here we could rest in peace on half decent beds and could indulge ourselves in some decent food. Some 24 hours later officers of the R.A.F. Regiment arrived at the camp to inform us that 'planes would soon be coming to drop by parachute food, clothes and medical supplies. It was not long before we saw Dakota 'planes circling above and around Saigon City and the outskirts, and we could plainly see the parachutes with canisters attached, falling not far from our camp. This was, of course, one more sign that we were nearing the freedom and civilization that had been taken from us three and a half years before. Now, with the arrival of our own military forces and with them those medical supplies of which our sick had been deprived during imprisonment, spirits rose rapidly.

Soon we were hungrily enjoying good food again. Our cooks, who had done marvellously well concocting meals from rice under extreme conditions, were now able to serve up decent meat and vegetables, and even specialities made from flour. Although we were certainly grateful for these most essential items, when we paraded for the issue of the clothes which had been dropped from the 'planes - surprise, surprise - jungle green uniform was produced! What irony. This was the uniform we should have gone into battle with at Singapore, not the sand-coloured / khaki drill that we had been issued with before leaving England and which was useless in the jungle environment.

It did not take us long to get used to our new lifestyle and we began to thoroughly enjoy freedom from guards watching over us. Arrangements had been made for a system of cash payment to be made to all ranks and so groups of us journeyed into Saigon City where visits were made to restaurants for meals and drinks.

Preparing ourselves for these excursions into Saigon now that we possessed new Army uniform of sorts, necessitated paying attention to our overall looks. Not having troubled nor concerned ourselves as to the style of our hairdressing whilst prisoners, and now about to go out on the town, we acquired some pork fat from the cookhouse and plastered it on our heads in the fashion of the Brylcreem days. We may have looked the part of smart, cared-for men as we set out on our walk to the City, but very soon we were belaboured by thousands of flies attracted by the smell of our pork-flavoured 'hair cream'.

FACE OF ADVERSITY

CHAPTER NINETEEN

OUT ON THE TOWN
– MEETING NEW FRIENDS
THEN HOMEWARD BOUND

It was after one such trip into Saigon, on returning with two friends to barracks, that the family of a French Indo-Chinese children's doctor, (Doctor Tran van Doc.) befriended the three of us. As a result we were invited to dinner at the family home, a large brick-built house situated just outside the City where we were hosted quite lavishly. After a wonderful meal and drinks with this family of six, (father, mother, a son and three daughters), we were asked if we would like to stay the night. We accepted the offer and soon we were enjoying the long-lost comfort of sleeping on real mattresses and pillows, under clean white sheets and protected from mosquitoes by white mosquito nets. Whilst here we heard for the first time in years, radio news programmes and broadcast music. Next morning the three of us enjoyed a wonderful breakfast of fried eggs and bacon, (another first for years), afterwards having to say our farewells to this kind and sympathetic family with promises to keep in touch when we were back home.

There is no doubt that our good fortune in meeting this lovely family, although only briefly, was instrumental in assisting us to realise that civilization was not lost. We would remember for always the genuine inquisitiveness of the parents, their son Georges who was in his early twenties, Janine age 18 years, Monique age 16 and Denise 15 years old. Fortunately the whole family was well versed in English and so we had no difficulty in understanding and answering the many questions they posed, their main interest being about our own families and life back home in England.

We would also remember the balmy evening after our meal, sitting in the rocking chairs on the veranda, the girls waving fans in front of us to keep us cool and to thwart the mosquitoes which were active around the open veranda. We were certainly lapping up this attention which was being foisted upon us, and although during most of this time the moments were so peaceful, now and again the tranquility was disturbed by spasmodic rifle fire in the area. These interruptions were caused by the actions of a few Vietnamese rebels in a show of opposition to the reassembling of their French, pre-Japanese rulers.

Despite this, it did not detract from the pleasantries we were enjoying with our kind, new friends of Saigon, French Indo-China who were helping us to obliterate the bad memories of the past.

MEETING NEW FRIENDS THEN HOMEWARD BOUND

The next day - it was now 12th September 1945 - was to be the time when we were to begin our long journey home. We were taken by lorries to Saigon airfield and there we boarded R.A.F Dakota 'planes, the same aircraft that had brought us food, medicines and clothes a few days earlier. The prospect of flying for the first time in our lives, and as far as I can recall this was to be a new experience for us all, there appeared to be no apprehension as we settled ourselves in the hard seats which ran along the length of each side of the 'plane.

Doctor Tran van Doc and his family

Naturally our feelings and thoughts at this time were that the war for us was now over, we were free at last from an unforgettable internment and we were taking off for home. But we were remembering those comrades and friends - all heroes - who were not with us.

The first leg of our journey, a flight of some 3 hours, took us to Bangkok where we alighted from the 'plane to be met by Red Cross personnel who tended those men who were still in need of medical attention, after which the remainder of us were also given a health check. Soon we were all sitting down to a meal in a marquee on the airfield, being given cigarettes, beer and chocolate and generally being pampered and fussed over. We were accommodated overnight at the airfield and next morning boarded our 'plane bound for Rangoon, Burma, the next lap of our homeward journey. This flight took us over the northern part of the Burma/Thai railway, unrecognisable from the air, but still a grim reminder of the enforced labour that had caused so much suffering and loss of life in the building of it. It was a miracle that anybody had survived that terrible ordeal where men had been forced to labour on a starvation diet, driven on by brutality and suffering deprivation of medical help. As we looked down on that jungle where so many of our brave comrades had so painfully and unnecessarily died, we all gave thanks for our survival.

On landing at Rangoon airfield we received a welcome similar to that, which had been accorded us at Bangkok, the Red Cross again being prominent in giving sympathetic assistance to those in need. We were taken to an army barracks where we stayed for a couple of days, during which time we made a brief visit into

MEETING NEW FRIENDS THEN HOMEWARD BOUND

Rangoon. Later at the barracks Lord Louis Mountbatten who was Britain's Supreme Allied Commander, South East Asia, visited us and he declared to us that the Japanese would assuredly get their just deserts for the inhuman treatment which they had inflicted upon us all.

The next step of our homeward journey was anticipated with great enthusiasm, it was to be a journey by sea, which was to be the final lap from imprisonment to freedom. We were taken to Rangoon docks where we boarded a Polish ship the "Indrapoera". This was a fairly large vessel, but not in the luxury class of the American troopship which had taken us to our doom in 1942. Nevertheless, nobody was complaining, it was comfortable, food was good and plentiful, and there were sweets, chocolate and cigarettes in abundance. We were also given the opportunity to send telegrams to our families giving them news of our release from captivity and details of our journey homewards.

So the seaward and last leg of our journey began, sailing from Rangoon and out into the Bay of Bengal and thence southwards to Ceylon where, on 27th September, our ship dropped anchor in the harbour at Colombo. We were permitted to spend two or three hours shore leave at Colombo, liberty boats being available to those of us who wished to take the opportunity. A number of us accepted the offer and enjoyed the short trip in the liberty boat to the port of Colombo. We were interested in the local shops and people, and took advantage of the chance to see yet another country on what was proving to be almost a 'round the world trip'.

We returned to the ship and soon were on our way again heading West into the Arabian Sea towards the Gulf of Aden, the Red Sea and then through the Suez Canal to Port Said. The ship sailed on into the Mediterranean, eventually dropping anchor in the Strait of Gibraltar where we had a wonderful view of the Rock. There was to be no shore leave here, and early the next morning, 9th October, we set sail again preparing ourselves for what was expected to be a rough passage through the Bay of Biscay. We had noticed that the deck rails of the ship had safety storm nets attached, which, we were told, was an indication that rough seas were anticipated. As it turned out, we were not unduly troubled by the weather here and soon we were nearing the English Channel.

FACE OF ADVERSITY

XX

CHAPTER TWENTY

HOME AGAIN
– THANKFUL FOR SURVIVAL
AFTER FOUR LOST YEARS

At long last, on 18th October 1945, the ship docked at Southampton where we were welcomed on the dockside by the band of the Royal Marines who played us off the ship with rousing military music and some modern tunes, which of course we had never heard before. Setting our feet on English soil again now in October 1945, exactly 4 years after leaving on that fateful trip thousands of miles away, was an unbelievable experience. Each of us was appreciative of all the help, sympathy and care that had been given to us since our release from captivity and now we were looking forward to joining our families. First we were taken to an army transit camp where we were fed, issued with new army battle dress and given railway warrants for our journeys home.

Arriving at Cambridge railway station the next day was a quiet homecoming really, we were not expecting a welcoming party as only two or three of us on that particular trip had been together when we had journeyed to North Walsham to join the army in February 1940. We bade farewell to each other, arranging to meet for a beer or two at a later date and promising never to find employment building railways, nor eating meals which contained rice !

When I reached my home I saw that a large "Welcome Home" poster had been strung across the front of our house. This was the moment that we all had hoped and longed for, but so many times during the past years an occasion which most of us thought would not happen, and we who had survived to enjoy the moment could not, and would not forget those thousands of our comrades who had bravely and involuntarily succumbed because of the inhumanity of the Japanese.

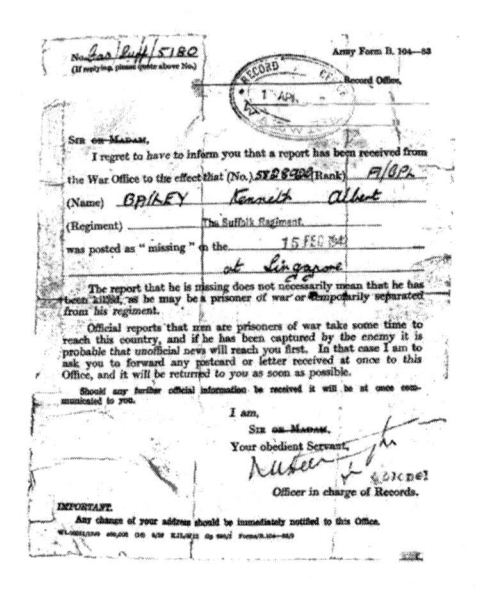

In compiling this story, forever thankful for my survival from that period of my life as a prisoner of war, I owe much to many people, not least to my wife Pearl to whom I have been married for 54 years having met her when I was stationed in Liverpool. Without Pearl and our three children with their sympathy and tolerance, especially during the times of my sickness and spells in hospitals, I might not have found the ability to withstand the strains of settling back into civilisation again. As much can be said also of others, such as doctors and medical specialists, especially those at the former Royal Air Force Hospital at Ely, who tended and investigated hundreds of returned former Far East prisoners of war who were still suffering both mental and physical suspected tropical-related ailments. My appreciation too, extends to the many post-war work colleagues, together with members of my leisure and sports clubs teams who often had to "carry" me through games when I was not up to true fitness. This friendly help over the years has enabled me, sometimes in sufferance, to maintain my urge to try to forget the years when I and my fellow prisoners were so incapacitated as to yearn for just a few minutes respite from slavery.

At times it seems difficult to forget the sinister years as prisoner of the Japanese, and then as I look through the few items of memorabilia in my possession, such as the remains of my diary for

HOME AGAIN – THANKFUL FOR SURVIVAL AFTER FOUR LOST YEARS

1942, and the telegrams sent by the Army Records Office to my parents notifying them of my being "missing" and then later that I was a prisoner of war, gives some gratification that someone was at least in touch with my family on my behalf. Other items of memorabilia such as the telegrams from the Records Office in-

Copy of army telegram notifying that I was a P.O.W in Japanese hands

forming my family that I had been released from captivity, and cablegrams sent by me from ports of call on the seaward journey home must have given great relief and hope to them, as it certainly gave to me, that we had better times to look forward to. Amongst other items which bring back those memories of the past, is the 'Welcome Home' letter received in September 1945 by all former Far East prisoners of war from His Royal Highness King George VI.

HOME AGAIN – THANKFUL FOR SURVIVAL AFTER FOUR LOST YEARS

BUCKINGHAM PALACE

The Queen and I bid you a very warm welcome home.

Through all the great trials and sufferings which you have undergone at the hands of the Japanese, you and your comrades have been constantly in our thoughts. We know from the accounts we have already received how heavy those sufferings have been. We know also that these have been endured by you with the highest courage.

We mourn with you the deaths of so many of your gallant comrades.

With all our hearts, we hope that your return from captivity will bring you and your families a full measure of happiness, which you may long enjoy together.

George R.I.

September 1945.

Copy of 'welcome home' message from King George VI in September 1945

FACE OF ADVERSITY

POSTSCRIPT

Although this is a personal testimony of three and a half years as a prisoner of the Japanese, it is a story which could be similarly related by thousands of men who had been taken from carefree civilian lives in 1940, to the strictly disciplined environment of conscripted military service and thence to humiliation, incarceration and degradation as prisoners of war under the fiendish Japanese Imperial Army.

Those who were lucky to survive through the starvation, cruelty and deprivation, through sickness and disease, could rightly say that even those dreadful experiences had been of some value. The comradeship and faith under appalling conditions, when the best and the worst elements of human nature were revealed, helped in keeping each other alive. That same spirit still exists. The memories of friends who had suffered, and seen others struggling to pull through have been instrumental in keeping those brotherhoods as close today as before, as have the world-wide military reunions and ex-prisoner of war clubs. Apart from these friendships, on a personal note, the meeting with the French-Indo Chinese family at Saigon on our release from captivity has given my family pleasant contact by way of greetings at Christmas each year, and on one occasion a very special reunion in London.

Reflecting on the circumstances which led to the disaster that befell the thousands of Allied troops who were eventually, but quickly left isolated and almost unaided at Singapore in January 1942, it was known to us all at the time, as it must also have been known by those in supreme command, that we were "lambs being led to the slaughter." This was an experience of which we would not want reminding, for after training to be soldiers for two years, travelling on the high seas for three and a half months and 20,000 miles, it was humiliating to survive in battle for just a fortnight in the defence of the supposedly "strongest British bastion east of Suez," the impregnable "Fortress Singapore." Those of us sent to Singapore in the early days of 1942 were without doubt, badly and sadly let down, being left abandoned like thousands of "sitting ducks" without the necessary resources with which to put into practice that which we had been trained to do for our country.

Now, safely back again in "civvy street," I have to be grateful for survival after suffering twenty-two relapses of Benign Tertian malaria between January 1943 and August 1945, Bacillary dysentery, Beriberi and Jaundice x 3. Although down to just over 9 stones weight after work on the infamous railway, quite soon after arrival home in 1945 I had piled on weight to my heaviest ever - an unhealthy 14 stones. This rather sudden increase in weight was due no doubt to the rapid and large intake of rich food on release after three and a half years of non-nutritional food. My gross 14 stones weight was quickly reduced to normality by sensible eating and healthy exercise, together with peace of mind that the appallingly bad times were past and could never return.

Although life as a prisoner of the Japanese - wherever the eventual destiny - could only have been a life of hell, the jungle camps of Thailand were places of complete and utter indecencies. The enforced labour in building the railway from Thailand to Burma was slavery, which alone killed off many colleagues, as did the sadistic acts of cruelty inflicted by the Japs. The inadequate diet of rice, with very little else, resulted in many serious ailments so that men suffering from malaria, dysentery, beriberi and cholera were toiling under terrible strain with no hope of sympathy, compassion or medical aid from our captors. The monsoon rains which fell for much of the time, and the oppressive tropical heat, did little to give any respite from work. The railway had to be built no matter what. Nor was there any comfort inside the camp huts when the rain leaked through the sparse attap roofing. The emaciated bodies lying on the bamboo bed spaces, not only having to contend with the damp and cold, but were also at the mercy of bloodsucking bed bugs and irritating lice.

The huts designated for the care and so-called treatment of the very sick were exactly the same in structure as the others in all the camps; with the same uncomfortable split bamboo bed spaces, lice, bugs and inadequate protection from mosquitoes. Although referred to as 'hospital' huts, they were far from being places where sick civilized human beings could be given decent nursing care in spite of the supreme dedication shown by medical officers and their helpers in extremely squalid conditions and with lamentably deficient medical supplies.

All of these things, together with the filthy, maggot-ridden latrines that existed in all the jungle railway camps, and especially the lack of that essential medical treatment, were conditions that survival from could only be ascribed to the supernatural. Today, some 58 years after the horrors of the jungle railway began - the enormity of which was immense - many times it is difficult to believe that one had been there and was alive to tell the tale.

In these modern times when circumstances cause to bring past memories flooding back, I am sure that all who survived the jungle incarceration, recall more than anything else, the suffering of comrades in those dreadful hospital huts. Comparisons are naturally made with present-day hospital conditions where patients and hospital staff are in appropriate, decent surroundings. Nevertheless, and quite naturally perhaps, there appear to be grounds sometimes, for faultfinding even in such conditions. Those of us who saw and suffered illness and disease in the jungle, to afterwards lose patience sometimes whilst waiting for attention in hospitals or doctors' surgeries nowadays, soon return to sanity and appreciation for our existence.

Although time is said to be a great healer, that awful period of imprisonment has left so many nasty and ugly wounds, the scars from which will never disappear. For most of the survivors, physical and mental suffering has never ceased. There are those whose limbs will never allow them to walk well again, and men with sight and hearing impaired. The thousands who went through the pains of dysentery in the jungles, despite much sympathetic attention by their own general practitioners on returning home, and with modern medical innovations, still have intestinal weaknesses that from time to time erupt to bring back, not only pain, but also embarrassment, traumatic memories and anxieties. Without exception, the after-effects of malarial fevers still, and forever will, cause nightmarish dreams as reminders of terrifying experiences of captivity. Those of us who still suffer from these uncontrollable disturbances of the mind during sleep, experience some stress in struggling to awaken oneself from these paralytic-like sensations.

Whilst survival from such a revolting experience, and the subsequent return to civilisation is looked upon as a merciful and thankful reprieve, those men who did not return from that jungle of hell, died as a direct result of Japanese inhumanities in barbarous ill-treatment, and failure to provide decent food and medical help in accordance with the 1907 Hague Convention. The Japanese, who signed that convention, did nothing to protect prisoners in any way as the convention provides a party to it should. The fact that prisoners working on the Thai/Burma railway were denied adequate medical treatment by their captors, amounted to gross non-conformity of a ruling that stated that a party to the convention must also protect prisoners it has captured, and if the case so demands, be liable to pay compensation.

There are without doubt thousands of other persons who were persecuted as a result of being caught up in the occupation of their countries by the Japanese and, so being interned, and sometimes being forced to work in the same way as prisoners of war, are also deserving of recompense. American history books record that even Japanese residents in the U.S.A. at the outbreak of World War II, after internment, were compensated for lost liberty and property, and not necessarily as a result of any ill-treatment as was the case of Japanese prisoners of war, and those others who suffered at the hands of the Japanese.

Concerning compensation, in these present times when huge sums of money are paid out to claimants - in some cases for so-called post-traumatic stress brought on by relatively minor happenings or sufferings - it seems that the fighting men of the Allied countries, for whom they had represented and afterwards suffered for as prisoners of the Japs, received, in comparison, a mere pittance from the proceeds of the sale of Japanese assets seized at the outbreak of war. Not only did prisoners of the Japanese suffer mentally and physically during the years of incarceration, they never stopped suffering at all after the end of the war when most were still young. All those sufferings could be traced back to prison camp days, the reality of which bears no comparison - with all due respect to those genuine cases - to the pitiful claims made by some of today's supposedly stressed out weaklings of society who have neither self-respect nor pride. In many such cases, some claimants who, unlike those who were forced to serve their country during wartime, had opted to take up their particular employment and then, with feeble excuses for not being able to complete their full commitment to their chosen jobs, plead for compensation.

Although former Far East Prisoners of War who returned home were thankful for their survival from such an ordeal, the families of those who did not return should have received some recompense, the loss of their loved ones being wholly due to the Japanese disregard of Convention Rules appertaining to protection of war prisoners. Those prisoners who did not survive captivity died because they were deprived of reasonable food and medicines, forced to work under appalling conditions and physically ill treated by the Japanese. Because of those deprivations, many of the captives who had once weighed anything from eleven to thirteen stones, were reduced to merely skin and bone weighing only six or seven stones, and still being forced to labour despite suffering chronic illness and disease. In such circumstances, those prisoners who died were killed by, and because of Japanese neglect, as assuredly as if they had been executed by them.

> IN HONOURED REMEMBRANCE OF THE FORTITUDE AND
> SACRIFICE OF THAT VALIANT COMPANY WHO PERISHED
> WHILE BUILDING THE RAILWAY FROM THAILAND TO BURMA
> DURING THEIR LONG CAPTIVITY
> THOSE WHO HAVE NO KNOWN GRAVE ARE COMMEMORATED
> BY NAME AT RANGOON SINGAPORE AND HONG KONG AND
> THEIR COMRADES REST IN THE THREE WAR CEMETERIES
> OF KANCHANABURI CHUNGKAI AND THANBYUZAYAT
> *I will make you a name and a praise among all people of the earth
> when I turn back your captivity before your eyes, saith the LORD*

KEN'S DIARY
1942

AHMADNAGAR, INDIA

PAGES PRIOR TO
AND DURING CAPTIVITY

JANUARY

Thursday January 8th
Battalion route march

Friday January 9th
Field training and guard mounting. A few of us went to the town bazaar in the evening, had a rotten time.

Saturday January 10th
Company drill – nothing much doing. Terrible life.

Sunday January 11th
Went to church service. A lovely day. Moping all day. Life is terribly lonely.

Monday January 12th
Field training and cleaning guns afternoon, then slept.

Tuesday January 13th
Getting packed up to move. Busy day.

Wednesday January 14th
Left Ahmadnagar, walked to station. Left by train, travelled all night.

Thursday January 15th
Arrived at Bombay at 12.30pm; had dinner at 1 o'clock. Boarded boat at 2 o'clock. Had good meal at 7.30pm.

Friday January 16th
Still anchored in harbour. Writing to Mum & Ruby. Layed up deck afternoon with G I (?)!

Saturday January 17th
Sent cablegram to Mum, also air mail card. Rumours of shore leave.

Sunday January 18th
Church service. Small ship on fire. Alarm sounded.

Monday January 19th
Anti-aircraft lecture. Alarm in afternoon, stood by guns. Dreamed of home. Left B..... (Bombay) 1300hrs.

KEN'S DIARY 1942

JANUARY

Tuesday January 20th
Lovely day. Well out to sea now. Alarm sounded.

Wednesday January 21st
Choppy sea, windy, sun shining. Battalion lecture by Major Watts.

Thursday January 22nd
Major Watts lecture. Slept and then played cards. Played cards in evening again. Escort joined us.

Friday January 23rd
Dangerous waters.
Getting very warm again.
Sat on deck before tea.

Saturday January 24th
Wrote to Ruby and Fred.

Sunday January 25th
Church parade on open deck. Slept on deck.

Monday January 26th
Anti-aircraft duty commences tomorrow.
Getting near destination.

Tuesday January 27th
A/A duty started.
Expecting some excitement.
Entered Banka Straits.
Raining like hell all night.
Catalinas escorting

Wednesday January 28th
Rather dull. One hour ahead of schedule. Bombed by lone plane – driven off.

Thursday January 29th
Arrived at S...... (Singapore). Air raids. Went to camp – on guard all night.

Friday January 30th
Not much doing.
Orders to move.

Saturday January 31st
Left camp. Bombed all around. Not much excitement – yet! Arrived at Pongool Point. 7 o'clock. Rained all time whilst marching.
Dug in straight away.

FEBRUARY

Sunday February 1st
Nothing much doing – still digging in and waiting. A lovely day.

Monday February 2nd
Moved into new position. Digging all night. Slept all day.

Tuesday February 3rd
Another positional move. Malaya taken by Japs.

Wednesday February 4th
Digging again - and all night. Dull day.

Thursday February 5th
Shelled from mainland 7.30am. Rotten time!

Friday February 6th
Shelled again. Things now warming up. Most of the day in shelter.

Saturday February 7th
Breakfast interrupted by a few shells – continuing

Sunday February 8th
Nothing much doing and still digging and waiting. Grand day. Sitting in armchair on verandah – peaceful now. Terrific duel at night until 2400 hours. Japs landed on west Coast at 2400 hours.

Monday February 9th
Moved into another position. Digging all night, slept all day. Lovely day. Tired as hell. Moved back for rest at 9 o'clock.

Tuesday February 10th
Moved again. Rather dull. News not so good.

Wednesday February 11th
Digging again – all night. Rather dull all day. Weather good. Wiring on coast all night. Bombardment at intervals.

Thursday February 12th
Shelled from mainland 7.30am. Having a rotten time. Slept morning. Moved to front 5 o'clock.

FEBRUARY

Friday February 13th
Shelled again – getting hotter. Most of day spent in shelter. Plenty of action

Saturday February 14th
Breakfast interrupted by a few bombs – continuing. Same again. Nerve racking business.

Saturday February 15th
Raffles College. War finished. Plenty of food – and whisky!

Monday February 16th
Good breakfast. Saw first Jap at breakfast time. Handed over all weapons etc. Slept out in open.

Tuesday February 17th
Leaving today at 5 o'clock. Slept along roadside at night. Continued march at 06.30

Wednesday February 18th
Arrived at Changi at 11 o'clock. Very good barracks.
Thursday February 19th
Shortage of food. Went swimming in afternoon.

Friday February 20th
Still existing – somehow! Everybody hungry. Swimming in afternoon.

Saturday February 21st
Swimming again today. Life is rather empty.

Sunday February 22nd
Very fine today. Church parade 11 o'clock. Swimming at 4 o'clock.

Monday February 23rd
Same old life. Fine day today. Swimming at 4 o'clock.

Tuesday February 24th
Swimming 4 o'clock. Nothing much doing. Rice being issued now by Japanese.

Wednesday February 25th
Parade for Japanese C in C. No swimming today. More rice!

FEBRUARY & MARCH

Thursday February 26th
Lovely day after night of rain. Rainy season setting in.

Friday February 27th
Swimming 1015 – lovely day. Still plenty of rice!

Saturday February 28th
Rained afternoon. No swim today. Rice all meals. Rumours of spiritualistic forecasts of returning to neutral country or home on March 29th!

Sunday March 1st
Dreamed last night of Ruby. Lovely morning. Church parade. Rained all afternoon – slept most of time.

Monday March 2nd
Raining first thing – off and on all day. Reading most of afternoon. Getting rather fat on rice!

Tuesday March 3rd
Quite nice day today. Rained on way to swimming – swam in oil! Porridge for breakfast. Tried to sleep in afternoon – in vain.

Wednesday March 4th
Went scrounging in morning. Read all afternoon. Still plenty of rice (had first taste of bread for a fortnight – grand)

Thursday March 5th
Lovely day. Sat talking all morning, reading in afternoon – not many books here. Still waiting for Sunday 29th!

Friday March 6th
Lovely day. Reading all day. More bread today. (Rolls).

Saturday March 7th
Rather dull today first thing. Rissole and rice and tea – breakfast. Rice and curry and tea – dinner. Rice and dripping – supper. Moving some of kit to new camp – got soaking wet in terrific downpour.

KEN'S DIARY 1942

MARCH

Sunday March 8th

Rice and cheese (1/24th) and tea – breakfast. Rice, jam and tea – dinner. Rice, jam, dumpling, peas and tea – supper. Moved to new camp. Had to build own bivouacs.

Monday March 9th

Breakfast 7.30 – rice, stew and tea. Left for Singapore 9 o'clock. Lunch (very small) on roadside. Rice biscuit and 1/24th cheese.
Arrived at camp.

Tuesday March 10th

Started work at High School clearing up clothing etc; treated very well by Japanese. Arrived back at 5.15.

Wednesday March 11th

Same place and job. Once again treated by Japanese like own countrymen!!
Had enjoyable day.

Thursday March 12th

Same place today. Quite good day. More rumours!!!

Friday March 13th

Same place again.
Raining all day.

Saturday March 14th

Last day of work at same place. Left at 6 o'clock. Sorry to leave after being in such good company.

Sunday March 15th

Resting today.
Preparing to move back.

Monday March 16th

Moving at 11 o'clock. Left at 12 o'clock. Raining nearly all the way. Arrived back at 6 o'clock. Rained all night.

Tuesday March 17th

Raining again today.
Had good night's sleep, under bivouac.

Wednesday March 18th

Fine first thing – looks promising. Rain has started and we are once more crouched under our bivouacs. Raining most of night.

MARCH & MAY

Thursday March 19th
Woke up by downpour of rain at 8 o'clock. Got up at 8.45. Water carrying at 9 o'clock in the rain. Reading in afternoon. Tent waterlogged.

Friday March 20th
Quite nice this morning, but a few clouds about. No rain all day. 29th drawing near.

Saturday March 21st
Fine again today. Plenty of rumours.

Sunday March 22nd
Fine but a few clouds. Rather close. Not feeling too fit today. Still eating rice. More rumours. Reading all afternoon, our only enjoyment.

Monday March 23rd
Fine again. Feeling much better today.

Tuesday March 24th
First thing weather fine; remained fine all day.

Wednesday March 25th
Fine first thing. Rain in afternoon.

Diary pages lost between March 25th and 29th April 1942

Thursday April 30th
Working again. More rain. Plenty of good rumours!

Friday May 1st
RUBY'S BIRTHDAY
Grand morning – more rain!

Saturday May 2nd
Fine to start with, but rain during afternoon. Work as usual.

Sunday May 3rd
Staying in camp today. Lovely morning. Out in afternoon clearing houses for more prisoners.

Monday May 4th
Out working again – road making.

KEN'S DIARY 1942

MAY

Tuesday May 5th
Work again today on lorries – easy day.

Wednesday May 6th
Working again today. Raining all morning.

Diary pages lost between 6th and 21st May

Thursday May 21st
Fine today. NO WORKING PARTY today. Did a little work around the camp. Slept in afternoon. No rations up yet.

Friday May 22nd
Working around camp. No rations yet. Rations arrived at 6 o'clock.

Saturday May 23rd
Fine again.
Rumours of air activity during night.
Yorkshire pudding – breakfast.
Yorkshire pudding – supper.

Sunday May 24th
Day of rest.
Yorkshire pudding – breakfast. Lovely day. Meat, potato Patty – supper and rice of course.

Monday May 25th
Burnt rice – breakfast.
Working around camp.
Very dull today.
Burnt rice – dinner.

Tuesday May 26th
No working party. Fine day.

Wednesday May 27th
Working parties starting. Stayed in camp. New division of Japs taking over.

Thursday May 28th
Went out working, got wet through as it rained all the time. Arrived back at 4 o'clock. Rations becoming short again. Rations arrived during evening.

MAY & JUNE

Friday May 29th
Stayed in camp, not much work to do. Good supper — rice, Yorkshire, meat stew and beans.

Saturday May 30th
On house patrol. Easy day. Baked rice and curry for breakfast; baked rice and pineapple for tea; meat roll and veg stew.

Sunday May 31st
On working party — more rain. Curry rice (breakfast). Plain rice (dinner), Yorkshire, veg and meat stew and cucumber.

Monday June 1st
Japanese day of prayer. Holiday for prisoners.

Tuesday June 2nd
Stayed in camp — quite an easy day. Plenty of vegetables etc being issued. Food improved. Had boiled egg and bread for supper.

Wednesday June 3rd
Stayed in camp again. Pay arrived at 4 o'clock.
DERBY DAY

Thursday June 4th
Working party.
Had very bad day again.
Stew, veg and rice — dinner

Friday June 5th
In camp. Curry and rice (breakfast).
Meat roll and veg — (dinner)
Midday. Plain rice.

Saturday June 6th
On working party. Good food now — egg and toast — supper. Pineapple, stew.

Sunday June 7th
Working party today, back at 5 o'clock. Stew and rissole (breakfast)
Midday (plain rice).
Dinner (Yorkshire and veg stew).
Supper — eggs.

KEN'S DIARY 1942

JUNE

Monday June 8th

JAPANESE DAY OF PRAYER
Rissole, rice and veg stew (breakfast)
Rice potato and tea (Midday)
Rice, meat pudding and stew (dinner)
Eggs, bread and rice (supper)

Tuesday June 9th

Day in camp. Not much work.
Meat, rissole, stew and rice (breakfast).
Fish cake, cucumber and rice (midday). Pudding, stew, veg and rice (dinner).
Beans on toast (supper).

Wednesday June 10th

Working party.
Finished at 6.30.
Meat, rissole, stew and rice (breakfast).
Baked rice (midday).
Meat patty, stew, rice and spuds (dinner). Fried eggs and bread (supper).

Thursday June 11th

Working party.
Rained a little.
Breakfast – rissole, rice and tea.
Dinner - baked rice.
Supper – pudding, stew, meat and rice.

Friday June 12th

Stayed in camp.
Rained most of day.
Breakfast - stew and rice.
Midday – baked rice.
Dinner – meat pudding, veg stew and rice. Supper – egg on toast.

Saturday June 13th

Working party.
Breakfast – stew and rice.
Midday – stew, rice, meat pudding and cucumber.
Dinner – Yorkshire, veg stew, rice and pineapple. Arrived back at 7 o'clock.

JUNE

Sunday June 14th

Working party. Arrived back at 7.15. Breakfast – stew and rice.
Midday – baked rice.
Dinner – fish cake, potato, meat turnovers, beans, spinach and rice.

Monday June 15th

Working party – arrived back at 7.30.
Breakfast – rice rissole, stew.
Midday – baked rice.
Dinner – meat pie, rice and stew.

Tuesday June 16th

Working party. Rained most of day. Arrived at camp at 6 o'clock.
Breakfast – veg stew and rice.
Midday – rice.
Dinner – pudding, meat stew and rice.

Wednesday June 17th

Working party in camp.
Breakfast – veg stew and rice.
Midday – rice and cucumber.
Dinner – meat pudding, veg stew and rice (very good!).
Rained nearly all night.

Diary pages lost between June 18th - 24th

Thursday June 25th

Stayed in camp. Washing in afternoon. Breakfast – rice and stew.
Midday – boiled rice.
Dinner – meat pie, potato, gravy and rice.

Friday June 26th

Weekly day of rest. Church service. Breakfast – rice and stew.
Midday – rice, cucumber and radish.
Lovely day – moved into new hut.

Saturday June 27th

No working party.
Breakfast – rice and gravy.
Midday – baked rice.
Dinner – meat pie, veg and rice.

Sunday June 28th

On working party. Easy day. Hottest day of year.
Breakfast – rice and gravy.
Midday – baked rice.
Dinner – brown stew, dumplings, veg and rice.

JUNE & JULY

Monday June 29th

Working party. Another easy day. Arrived back at 4.30pm. Breakfast – rice and gravy. Midday – boiled rice. Dinner – boiled pudding, rice, yam stew and rissole.

Tuesday June 30th

On working party. Very hot. Breakfast – rice and gravy. Midday – baked rice. Dinner – rice, stew, veg and meat patty.

Wednesday July 1st

On working party. Very hot. Breakfast – rice and stew. Midday – baked rice. Dinner – rice, meat roll, stew, potato and beans.

Thursday July 2nd

Working Party. Looks stormy – turned out very hot. Breakfast – rice and gravy. Midday – baked rice. Dinner – plain pudding, bean and veg stew and rice. Wrote home.

Friday July 3rd

Day of rest. Moved back again into huts. Breakfast – rice and gravy. Midday – rice and cucumber. Dinner – rice pudding, stew and yam.

Saturday July 4th.

Working Party. Breakfast – roasted rice. Midday – gravy, baked and boiled rice. Dinner – rice dumpling, stew and beans. Hot again. Dreamed of home and Ruby.

Sunday July 5th

Working Party. Looks fine early. Breakfast – rice biscuit and gravy. Midday – baked and boiled rice. Dinner – rice, boiled pudding, veg and stew.

Monday July 6th

Working Party. Raining today. Breakfast – rice and gravy. Midday – baked and boiled rice. Dinner – rice, pudding and veg stew.

Tuesday July 7th

Working Party. Quite fine although cloudy. Breakfast – rice and gravy. Midday – boiled and baked rice. Dinner – rice, meat pudding and veg stew.

JULY

Wednesday July 8th

Working Party. Hot again.
Breakfast – rice and gravy.
Midday – baked rice.
Dinner – rice, stew
and pudding.

Diary pages lost between 9th July and 13th August

Thursday August 13th

Still in camp. Rained morning.
Breakfast – rice and gravy.
Midday – baked and boiled
rice and cucumber. Dinner –
rice, veg and meat stew.

Friday August 14th

Breakfast (9 o'clock) – rice
and fish cake.
Midday – baked rice and gravy.
Dinner – rice, patty, veg stew.

Saturday August 15th

Have a pair of boots now
(of a kind).
Breakfast – rice and gravy.
Midday – baked rice and sugar.
Dinner – rice rissole, veg stew
and pudding. Had to hand
boots back – much too small.

Sunday August 16th

Once again in camp.
Breakfast – rice & gravy.
Midday – baked rice
and cucumber.
Dinner – rice, meat pudding,
veg stew.

Monday August 17th

As usual and completely
"browned" off". More rain.
Breakfast – rice and gravy.
Midday – baked and boiled rice.
Dinner – rice patty, veg stew.

Tuesday August 18th

Still bootless.
Breakfast – rice and gravy.
Midday – rice and cucumber.
Dinner – rice rissole, veg stew,
date pudding and white sauce!
BIG RACE TONIGHT.

Wednesday August 19th

Again in camp.
Breakfast – rice and gravy.
Midday – rice and cucumber.
Dinner – rice, meat pudding,
veg stew.
Have a pair of boots – again!

FACE OF ADVERSITY

ABOUT THE AUTHOR

Kenneth Albert George Bailey was born 6th November 1919 in Parkeston, Essex. He is the son of a London born police inspector, and at the age of 7 years moved with his family to Cambridge. Kenneth was educated at Brunswick Junior School, and from age 11 years at the Cambridge and County High School for Boys. His first job after leaving school at 16 years of age was as a tailor's assistant.

On 18th January 1940 was called up for National Service. On 27th October 1941, as a Corporal infantryman in 5th battalion Suffolk Regiment, he sailed to Singapore where, on 15th February 1942 he was captured by the Japanese. After three and a half years imprisoned in Singapore, Thailand and Indo-China, he was released in 1945.

In 1946 Kenneth joined the police force and married Pearl, a Liverpool girl whom he had first met when stationed in that city during 1941. Ken and Pearl have 2 sons and a daughter by their marriage.